The Courage to Be Yourself

The **Courage** to **Be Yourself**

AN UPDATED GUIDE TO EMOTIONAL STRENGTH AND SELF-ESTEEM

Sue Patton Thoele

Conari Press
Coral Gables, FL

Cover Design: Katia Mena
Layout & Design: Carmen Fortunato
Interior Illustrations: Sandie Turchyn
Author Photo: Luke Landin

For permission requests, please contact the publisher at:
Mango Publishing Group
2850 S Douglas Road, 4th Floor
Coral Gables, FL 33134 USA
info@mango.bz

For special orders, quantity sales, course adoptions and corporate sales, please email the publisher at sales@mango.bz. For trade and wholesale sales, please contact Ingram Publisher Services at customer.service@ingramcontent.com or +1.800.509.4887.

The Courage to Be Yourself: An Updated Guide to Emotional Strength and Self-Esteem

Library of Congress Cataloging-in-Publication number: 2022913384
ISBN: (print) 978-1-68481-026-0, (ebook) 978-1-68481-027-7
BISAC: SEL023000, SELF-HELP / Personal Growth / Self-Esteem

Table of Contents

The Power of Thought   182

Yes, We Do Have Rights   196

CHAPTER FOURTEEN

Being a Loving and Accepting Friend to Yourself   213

Sharing the Journey

My heart swells with gratitude as I revisit *The Courage to Be Yourself*, to revise and update it for this Tenth Anniversary Edition. I'm grateful for all the people who from the very beginning encouraged me to write when I didn't have a clue how to begin or the confidence to believe that I had anything worthwhile to say. And most of all I'm grateful to the women who have read the book and, in doing so, have given it a life of its own.

Receiving letters and talking with these readers has been a continual and invaluable reminder to me that no matter how diverse we may seem, women share very similar journeys. In essence, we want and need to gather the courage to be whom we were born to be.

As is often the case, we teach what we most need to learn, and that was certainly true for me in writing *The Courage to Be Yourself*. The book emerged from my own struggles with fear, feelings of limitation, and the unrelenting criticism I heaped upon myself. Because I needed to practice the art of loving and being myself, this book was born. But it has survived and thrived because of you, the readers. Thank you from the depths of my heart!

Many of the women who first read the book are now mothers and grandmothers, and it's my hope and prayer that this revised edition will become a legacy they will want to pass on to their daughters and granddaughters.

The idea of writing *The Courage to Be Yourself* first occurred to me in the small groups and seminars that I and a dear friend, Bonnie Hampton, led for several years. As we explored women's issues—which included hopes, dreams, frustrations, fantasies, and fears—I was struck by the fact that whether married or single, stay-at-home moms or career women, old or young, the women in the groups struggled with similar anxieties and were saddled with comparable limiting beliefs. Amid both laughter and anguish, we helped each other transform common fears into the courage to express our authentic selves. Bonnie's and my goal was to provide simple but powerful tools for helping ourselves and participants enhance self-esteem and tap into our elusive but ever-present core of emotional strength.

I'm hoping the true stories and examples shared in *The Courage to Be Yourself* will act as a group experience for you to help you overcome any tendency you may have to undervalue yourself and to encourage you, instead, to fully love and appreciate how wonderful you really are. Sharing our journey with other women can uphold and sustain us as we find the courage to be uniquely ourselves and realize that emotional strength and self-esteem are, in fact, our birthright, our privilege, and our responsibility.

PART ONE

Finding the Courage to Be Yourself

CHAPTER ONE

AN EXPANDED VISION OF SELF

I want, by understanding myself, to understand others. I want to be all that I am capable of becoming.... This all sounds very strenuous and serious. But now that I have wrestled with it, it's no longer so. I feel happy—deep down. **All is well.**

KATHERINE MANSFIELD (LAST JOURNAL ENTRY)

Because we have learned so much, finding the courage to be ourselves may be easier for some of us now than it was fifteen years ago when I began writing the first edition of this book. Easier because many women are reveling in a greater sense of personal freedom and embracing a more expansive vision of themselves. While we can still fall prey to fears and beliefs that limit us, we have also become more psychologically aware and therefore better able to understand, move through, and overcome challenging feelings and circumstances.

That's the good news. The flip side is that finding and sustaining the courage to be ourselves continue to be a challenge for many women, myself included. Why is it still so darn hard?

One of the main reasons is that many of us were weaned on subtle and not-so-subtle innuendos regarding a "woman's role" and, as a result, were well trained to put ourselves last, if at all. Old, familiar habits and expectations such as these are not easily or quickly changed. Another deterrent to authenticity is the seemingly endless and ever expanding demands upon us. Over-commitment robs us of the time, energy, and interest necessary to ponder who we are and what we want or need.

It's true, we women are becoming increasingly independent and strong while continuing to love and support our friends, families, and communities. Ironically, the difficulty of being ourselves continues to be a common topic among women. Why do we so easily give ourselves away by doing more than we're comfortable doing? Why do we often succumb to the habit of devaluing ourselves and putting ourselves down? While no one is totally immune to the charm of outside approval, many of us are periodically mystified by the seemingly tenuous stability of our self-esteem and emotional well-being.

Most of us have spent a lot of time and effort redefining ourselves and discrediting inhibiting stereotypes. Given our hard and dedicated work to improve our feelings of self-worth, why is it so hard to hold on to a belief in ourselves when people react less than positively toward us? What causes our emotional strength to ebb away in the face of disapproval? Why does it take such effort for us to express what we really think and feel?

Faced with speaking my truth, especially if I fear it will lead to rejection of either myself or my ideas, often causes a lump to clog my throat and a heavy weight to settle on my heart. Am I a slow learner? Am I actually afraid of equality? Worse yet, am I an imposter?

No, I don't think so. And neither are you.

As the saying goes, we've come a long way. However, our training and socialization to accept second-class citizenry runs deep. And why wouldn't it? For millennia women have suffered punishments, ranging from denial of affection and support to being burned at the stake, for "stepping out of their rightful places." Given our history, it makes sense that a deep-seated fear of speaking our mind, being ourselves, and living our dreams is woven into the very fabric of our being. We now have the unprecedented opportunity to courageously recreate and reweave our lives and, consequently, the lives of our daughters and granddaughters.

Granted, many societal and individual assumptions are very different than they were a decade ago when this book was first published. However, under the seemingly solid ground of respect and equality that women have earned often lurks a quagmire of lingering patriarchal attitudes and desires.

Laura and Dan's story is a good example. As a young couple, their roles were traditional. Laura stayed home with their three children while Dan worked to support the family. When the children left home, Laura wanted to return to her career as a home decorator. Dan was all for it, or so they thought. Laura said to me, "You know, Sue, I believed him when he encouraged me to take the necessary classes and resume my career. So I was confused and angry when he put blocks in my way. First, he upped his requests for me to do errands for him, like going to the bank and cleaners and picking up stuff for his business. Then he had a series of little accidents and needed me to care for him." With a sigh, she continued, "I finally *got* it and asked him if, deep down, he resented my working. He denied it emphatically. But when he complained about never getting a good meal at home anymore, I knew that what he *thought* about my working was not what he *felt!*"

Luckily Laura and Dan have been able to work through this passage in their lives and consequently understand themselves and each other better. Dan was eventually able to see that, although he really wanted to support Laura's choice to work, he'd had a good thing going with a stay-at-home wife and felt abandoned when those perks diminished.

Change is hard for us all, men and women alike.

In fact, I have great compassion for both sexes as we weather the inevitable storms that accompany a change in paradigm. Thankfully many societies are now immersed in the process of converting from a patriarchal to an egalitarian paradigm. More simply put, we're transforming the model of Top Dog/Bottom Dog into Equal Partnership. In order to create and sustain these new cultural patterns we women must confront our own fears, including each tenacious tentacle that strangles our freedom to be ourselves. Not an easy task.

It's not easy for men or Top Dog–based organizations to adapt to the current necessary changes either. At the onset, women's increase in self-esteem and emotional strength can easily be perceived as a *de*motion in power and position to those accustomed to the loftiest perches on the pedestal. I clearly remember my husband, Gene, pensively lamenting, "I liked it the way it used to be!" That years-old memory makes me smile now. Then I wanted to snap, "Yeah, right! I'd like to have a wife like me, too!"

The beauty of finding the courage to face our fears and become ourselves is that everyone eventually wins. As an example, Gene and I are both happier as co-creators of a partnership than we ever were when he was the undisputed Top Dog. For me, life in general becomes sunnier and more fulfilled in direct proportion to my ability to overcome the hesitations I have about expressing my true self. Of course, I still struggle with certain fears, and I suspect that will always be true. But as I develop strength and confidence, my fears become much more manageable and far less paralyzing.

AWAKENING THE DIVINE FEMININE

One of the major areas in which our vision of self is expanding is in the spiritual realm. Myriad archeological discoveries, including goddess artifacts from ancient civilizations and the Dead Sea Scrolls, have opened our eyes to the esteem in which women were once held. Research has unearthed cultures that honored both the masculine and the feminine and recognized that each needed the other to create and sustain the greater whole. Interestingly, weapons were not found among the artifacts of these cultures, which suggests that ancient partnership societies rarely indulged in warlike activities. A state of affairs that pleased the Divine Feminine, I'm sure.

Our newborn awareness that feminine qualities were respected and revered in the past has allowed an expanded vision of ourselves to appear in the present, a vision that acknowledges Woman—or The Feminine—as deep, rich, wise, multidimensional, creative, lighthearted, and spiritual. This recognition and reclamation of The Feminine as invaluable and essential—even divine—is changing who we perceive ourselves to be. Is it possible that we are made in the image of a Mother God, a feminine creator, a divine spiritual essence? We're beginning to accept the answer as "yes."

Actually, the idea of feminine spirituality as Source, as well as Comforter, is an idea as old as time but one that has been essentially buried for centuries. In the minds and hearts of many people, and even some established religious traditions, the Divine Feminine—a spark of which resides at the center of all souls—is once again taking her place beside the Divine Masculine. For the good of ourselves, our families, and our very world, our mission is to become our true selves and in so doing awaken and express the Divine Feminine within.

QUALITIES OF THE DIVINE FEMININE

The Feminine is the embodiment of heart energy. Her key qualities are compassion and the ability to accept and honor the process of whatever is happening. Perhaps this is often easier for women because we are physically and emotionally programmed to honor the cycle of conception, pregnancy, and birth and to welcome and include whoever may be born from that long, mysterious process.

Contrary to the idea that women are overemotional, the Divine Feminine is well grounded emotionally and has the capacity to bring all of her energy to exactly where she is in the moment. Feminine energy accepts the paradoxes of life and has the ability to hold them within her heart simultaneously. Feminine energy connects deeply the Earth and all of her children, feeling for and with them.

The following list of feminine qualities—the vision of ourselves the Divine Feminine whispers in the stillness of our hearts—is by no means complete. You will be able to add many of your own.

THE DIVINE FEMININE IS...

Inclusive: recognizes the value and worth of all people and things

Honoring of process: is able to allow circumstances, ideas, and experiences to unfold

Empowered: with steeled softness, champions the weak and vulnerable and stands firm for what is right

Intuitive: is holistic, accessing immediate perception
rather than rational thinking

Compassionate: is empathetic, warm, open-hearted

Complementary: lives in concert with others, augmenting
the whole with her presence

Connective: desires to link hands and hearts

Cooperative: is able to work with others without needing
to be in control

Diffuse: perceives and understands a wide range of stimuli

Relational: is interested in preserving and
deepening relationships

Gentle: is able to live gently with herself and others

Receptive: is open to receive the new, different,
and wondrous

Empowering: awakens others to their potential

Forgiving: realizes that we are all imperfect and that non-
forgiveness dams the natural flow of spirit

Introspective: is drawn to the spiritual and
the philosophical

Healing: carries the ability to heal body, mind, and spirit
through talent for listening deeply to her internal,
inherent wisdom

Recognizing these qualities as ones that we possess, or can
aspire to possess, frequently helps us recognize and respect
our innate talent to usher in to all situations the energy of love
and acceptance. As with everything—and much to our chagrin
at times—the revolution of compassion, caring, and kindness
exemplified by the Divine Feminine needs to begin within
ourselves. As the song says, "Let there be peace on earth, and

let it begin with me." A revolution of love, a revolution of respect, a revolution of acceptance, tolerance, and inclusion. All of these values must first be nurtured in our own hearts and souls, and in our intimate social groups, if they are to be transformative for the whole. To begin this revolution of love, we need to brave our fears, extricate ourselves from the dung heap of disrespect and dismissal, and honor who we truly are.

FREEZE-DRIED FEMININE

In what was for me an eye-opening conversation, a dear friend was telling me that her adult daughter only seemed to relate to her when she needed something. "It's as if she freeze-dries me and puts me on a shelf until she needs something. Then she takes me down, reconstitutes me with her tears, and fully expects me to help her." I answered, "And you do, right?"

She moaned, "Yes..." and we laughed in recognition.

As I reflected on our talk, I realized that over the last several hundred years, our society, both consciously and unconsciously, has attempted to freeze-dry feminine energy and power, stow it safely in a corked jar, and bury it in the remote recesses of a dark cavern. As well as trying to silence women's intuition and wisdom, society has denigrated the Divine Feminine qualities of cooperation, inclusion, receptivity, and compassion, to name only a few, by relegating them to the second-class areas of servitude and sacrifice.

As sad as I am to admit it, the attempts to bury the innate spiritual qualities of the Divine Feminine were certainly successful with me. For many years, my sense of spiritual and personal power lay dormant, and I felt no sense of connection to the Divine Feminine or to the divinity within myself. Although I tried to act out feminine values by loving, caring, and supporting others, my service sprang mostly from fear and a sense of obligation rather than flowing freely from my heart. I did what I *should* do and neither embodied the values, spoke with the voice, nor radiated the joy of the Divine Feminine. She was asleep, freeze-dried in my heart, buried under mounds of false beliefs, societal injunctions, and visceral fears.

From talking with friends and working with clients, I know that my barren experience was not unique.

WAKE-UP CALLS

The Divine Feminine is issuing wake-up calls. And the most important of those calls are the ones stirring within our own hearts. Such stirrings may come in the form of little nudges to invoke a female power or deity while praying, intuitive flashes that we have the courage to voice and act upon, acts of kindness, love, and wisdom that effortlessly bubble from us, feeling intensely connected to nature, joyous bursts of creativity, or soft, silent whispers that come during dreams or meditation.

As we pay rapt and respectful attention to the whispers of the Divine Feminine within, we can usually find the courage to restructure our values around a core of compassion and connectedness toward both ourselves and others. Waking up to the Divine Feminine within our souls and then heeding her gentle pushes and pulls empowers us to live the expanded vision of self we are being shown. The invitation has been sent. With courage, commitment and intention, we can become our true selves: authentic, heart-centered women, light-bearers in our beleaguered world.

CHAPTER TWO

COURAGE: YOU HAVE IT!

I have met brave women who are exploring the
outer edges of human possibility, with no history to
guide them, and with a courage to make themselves
vulnerable that I find moving beyond words.

GLORIA STEINEM

Are you often filling the wants and needs of others without
having your own met? Do deadlines and difficult people
leave you feeling frazzled? Do you feel overworked and under-
appreciated? Do you grapple with self-limiting fears? Are you
more an enemy than a friend to yourself?

Despite the tremendous changes of the last fifty years and
the new vision of ourselves we've been given, many women will
still answer "yes" to the above questions. Often we are caught
in a tangled web of emotional dependence, afraid to express
who we really are.

EMOTIONAL STRENGTH AND SELF-ESTEEM

Emotional strength flows from a healthy and hearty sense of self-esteem. Emotionally strong women know themselves well, honor their strengths, nonjudgmentally work on their weaknesses, and treat themselves—and consequently others—with respect, understanding, and kindness. When a woman is emotionally strong, she is able to be gentle with herself and call upon her own inner core of strength as her main support even in the midst of chaos and failure.

For the vast majority of us, emotional strength and high self-esteem are attributes that we have worked diligently to attain, not ones that came easily or automatically. Courageously we build, balance, and stabilize our internal ego structure by overcoming one tiny—or tremendous—fear at a time and embrace a new vision of ourselves one insight at a time.

Uncovering, strengthening, and allowing our authentic self full expression is an ongoing, eternal process, a dance with our soul.

WHAT IS EMOTIONAL DEPENDENCE?

Emotional dependence is the opposite of emotional strength. It means needing to have others to survive, wanting others to "do it for us," and depending on others to give us our self-image, make our decisions, and take care of us financially. When we are emotionally dependent, we look to others for our happiness, our concept of "self," and our emotional well-being.

Such vulnerability necessitates a search for and dependence on outer support for a sense of our own worth.

Being emotionally dependent puts us at the mercy of our fears and other people's whims, and severely limits our freedom to be ourselves. Although our minds often know better, when we are emotionally dependent, we feel that others hold the key to our well-being, that they must know better than we do what is good for us. Or, we may believe that we must give ourselves away in order to gain and hold someone's love. That belief makes reassurance a necessity rather than a nicety.

Before I ever heard the term "emotional dependence," I knew that, in some mysterious way, I turned my life over to other people. It didn't really matter who they were—my parents, husband, kids, friends, coworkers. If they were happy with me, then I could be happy. If they approved of me, then I felt worthwhile. If they granted permission, then I believed it was okay for me to do or be something. I looked to others for approval before feeling confident enough to take a step or a stand. I wasn't myself; I was whoever I thought the person I was trying to please wanted me to be. Since I wasn't a mind reader, no matter what form I pretzeled myself into, I wasn't able to please everyone all of the time. But I tried. That's emotional dependence!

Denying or sacrificing ourselves on the altar of others' expectations—or what we perceive to be their expectations— leaves us with no *self*. Without an awareness of our self, the courage to express who we are, and the willingness to experience the discomfort and exhilaration that follows, we are not truly living. We are existing merely as mirrors, reflecting other people's lives. Until we are able to be our unique and beautiful (and, sometimes, ugly and mundane) selves, we cannot truly love either ourselves or others, and love is what life is all about.

Why do so many women have trouble maintaining emotional strength? As many researchers have shown, women have a deep need for emotional connectedness and intimacy. In fact, one of the premises of Carol Gilligan's book, *In A Different Voice,* is that women's voices are easily silenced by the culture because of their need for copacetic connectedness. This desire is not all bad, since it is what makes us such wonderful lovers, friends, and mothers. But when the need for connectedness is not balanced with the need to be our own person, we can become emotionally dependent, losing sight of ourselves and all our capabilities. We become afraid of anything that seems to threaten our relationships with others. Being disconnected can feel life threatening and is, therefore, terrifying to us. Out of our terror we often do exactly what we are afraid others will do—we abandon ourselves, littering the sides of our personal life-road with forsaken desires, goals, talents, and dreams.

Fear—of not being loved, of abandonment, of being thought to be selfish—is the main thing that keeps us vulnerable and bound in the chains of emotional dependence. Therefore, our two most difficult challenges are to truly believe it is okay for us to be ourselves and to learn to live with, move through, and heal our fears.

For many years, I was run by my fears. For example, I was deeply afraid of rejection or of offending anyone and would go to great lengths to avoid disagreement of any kind. But very few people who knew me would have said, "Wow, there's a woman who is really afraid!" I hid it well. And so, I was to learn, did countless other women.

Unfortunately, many of us have allowed fear to block our awareness of our inborn strengths. I myself used to be a master at doing that. Although other people perceived me as a strong and independent person, I frequently felt I was only playing at being grown-up. Others saw me as successful and mature, but inside, I felt buffeted by other people's moods. I knew that I hadn't taken responsibility for my own life, and I was afraid to do so.

Even though I had a master's degree in counseling and had been in private practice for several years, inwardly I felt I was "just a wife and mother." Sure, I had performed the work of an adult person, leading groups and seeing clients, but inside, I felt like a little girl dressing up and playing at these roles, hoping to gain the approval of others.

What changed? A great deal! I turned forty, met a wonderful woman friend who wouldn't let me lie to myself, and, most important, I began to really listen to myself. Each of us has a "still, small voice" inside that speaks to us continuously. The trouble is, we seldom listen. Yet, if we let it, our inner authentic self can guide us unerringly. You, too, can hear the voice inside you that will help you realize you have the courage to become who you really are.

I don't want to imply that I am now "fixed" and never wrestle with low self-esteem, because I do. There are times when I sink into vulnerability and inwardly protest that the consequences of being myself are too harsh and unfair. In reality, all my protests are not inner ones. I'm also prone to groan and moan outwardly and loudly to trusted friends when I'm feeling upset about something. Many of those grump-fests end in laughter, and it's with great relief that I can assure you that my painful stretches are not as long or hard as they once were. Sooner or later the lessons I've learned and the insights I've gained surface and act as a ladder to help me climb out of the pit. Growing through tough times and circumstances becomes easier and easier the more deeply I appreciate the fact that *not* being myself reaps the most serious consequences.

NOBODY SAID IT WOULD BE EASY

Courage is the willingness to act even when frightened. If we struggle with low self-esteem and have been emotionally dependent on others for a long time, it will be frightening to make independent decisions about our lives that may earn the disapproval of others. The only way to begin is by taking small steps that we can handle. Even a baby step puts us farther forward than no step at all. You'll be quite surprised at how much strength, confidence, and pride you get from tapping one little iota of your hidden inner courage.

Put a three-by-five card on your fridge, mirror, or in your wallet that says: **NOBODY SAID IT WOULD BE EASY!** Too often, we hold the underlying assumption that things *should* be easy, that if we face difficult challenges, it means we're somehow bad, or the world is against us. With either a judgmental or victim attitude, we find it all too easy to crumble and never discover how strong and creative we really can be. Change is rarely easy. But avoiding the difficulties in our lives never gives us the chance to conquer fear. When we overcome a fear or face challenges and win, we experience wonderful feelings of accomplishment and mastery.

It's important to free ourselves from the attitude that things should be easy, which only encourages us to resist difficulties. Shun the ain't-it-awful and woe-is-me attitudes in yourself and in other people. Negativity is highly contagious, so if at all possible avoid being around chronically negative people.

COURAGE:
AN EVERYDAY ACTUALITY

What exactly is courage? Courage is the ability to do what needs to be done, or feel what needs to be felt, in spite of fear. It's the willingness to risk or act even when we are frightened or in pain.

If you want to gain emotional strength and have more courage, you can. In fact, you already have a great deal of courage. We seldom think much about the courage we exert in simple, "normal" situations: having a baby, going to work day after day, sustaining relationships. It takes courage to fall in love, be honest with ourselves, survive a loss, move away from home, share a fear with a friend, ask for a raise, get a divorce, take on a job that challenges us, grow older, or tell someone when we're angry or hurt. Try writing down a list of things you've done even though you felt afraid. Those were acts of courage. Sometimes just getting up in the morning and proceeding with your life takes tremendous courage.

I hope it's clear by now that we already have courage. Being courageous, and moving toward a fuller realization of our own authentic self, is a natural process. What is it that keeps us from realizing our full, courageous potential? *Fear!* What do we fear? We fear the unknown, anything that has been painful for us in the past, or anything that feels different and risky.

Actually risk has an entirely different side too. With the right attitude, we can experience risk as exhilarating and creative. Risk is necessary for change, and change is necessary for growth. Growth is inevitable. We *will* grow, but will it be toward freedom or toward fearfulness? In order to be free, we need to learn to honor our fears but not allow them to control our lives.

Bringing our fears out into the open and talking honestly about them helps us work through them. An unspoken fear grows and gains force becoming much more powerful than one that is shared.

The trouble is, we're afraid to talk about our fears because we think others will see us as too emotional, immature, or foolish. So we keep quiet, thus creating a self-enclosed inner world in which we condemn ourselves for feeling as we do and believe we're the only fearful people we know. Our fear creates crippling isolation. But as we risk voicing our fear and find it accepted gently by others, it loses its power.

THE CO-DEPENDENT CAGE

In the decade since *The Courage to Be Yourself* was first published, much has been written and taught about emotional dependence, under the name "co-dependence." While co-dependence is often linked to being in a relationship with someone who is dependent on drugs or alcohol, it is far more pervasive than that. We can be co-dependent with our husbands, kids, co-workers—even our dog or parakeet.

Being co-dependent means we consistently put others' needs, wants, and demands before our own—in other words, emotional dependence. Instead of gaining our self-esteem, self-motivation, and self-worth from ourselves, we rely on others to provide those feelings for us. Quite a paradox: *self* as defined by *others.* When we turn our lives over to someone or something else, we are in a co-dependent cage. In that cage we become drugged by denial and depression.

If you feel that you have even a toe caught in the "co-cage," muster up your courage and find a friend or group of people who can help you work your way free. Recently I became aware that a dear friend was banging her head against the bars of a destructive marriage. Sadly she's been suffering in silence for several years and has gotten to the point where she fears for her mental and physical health. Although her husband isn't physically violent, his mental assaults are stripping away her emotional well-being and depleting her immune system. As a result, she is almost immobilized by depression and is plagued by illness after illness.

With encouragement from her therapist, myself, and a few friends, she has now broken her silence and is beginning to be honest about her situation. A courageous start. True freedom will be hers when she discovers the best way to escape from the very complicated co-dependent cage she is in.

Serving a life sentence as a co-dependent is tantamount to an emotional death penalty. Breaking out of the co-dependence cage is a life-giving escape. I have every confidence that you and my friend can do it. If I, who spent many years peering through the bars of co-dependence yearning for the freedom of emotional autonomy and independence, can do it, so can you.

FINDING THE WAY TO OURSELVES

We all know now that women have a tendency, in greater or lesser degrees, to be emotionally dependent in their relationships. But how do we free ourselves from the trap and enter into loving partnership instead?

I love the Irish proverb that says, "You've got to do your own growing, no matter how tall your grandfather was." It's true. We will do our own growing eventually, so let's not let fear seduce us into inaction. An excellent way to overcome the paralysis that often accompanies fear is to join a group of women who are working on issues similar to our own. If you are unable to find the help you need among your friends and family, there are co-dependency seminars and other support groups everywhere.

They can be found by inquiring at your local mental health department, checking with churches that often have lists of community services, or by asking friends.

In the seminars my partner, Bonnie, and I gave, the most important thing the women in them learned was to talk openly about their feelings. As we shared our shortcomings, secrets, fears, hostilities, joys, and disappointments, we realized we were not alone. Breaking out of isolation gives us permission to fully experience our feelings and then work through them.

Katy, a sweet, soft-spoken woman, sheepishly told me I couldn't possibly guess what she had discovered in one of our seminars. She was certain I'd be shocked and horrified to know that the main stress in her life related to her husband. Of course, I was neither shocked nor surprised. I know her husband, and he's a good man; but I also know that many women who are in relationships with good men feel stressed out. In Katy's case, the mere reassurance from another woman that she wasn't alone in her unrevealed feelings, and that she wasn't a terrible person for having them, gave her the freedom to accept what she was really feeling.

Knowing and accepting our true feelings is an essential step in moving beyond emotional dependence toward the ability to be ourselves. It takes an enormous amount of courage to be emotionally independent because we have been taught to believe that our natural role is as an adjunct to other people—a constant support, a helpmate, not an equal. However, with the advent of the partnership paradigm, the concept of inequality is obsolete. Having the courage to be who we really are is our natural birthright. If this is the case, then why is it so difficult for many of us to be ourselves, enjoy emotional independence, and have satisfying, equal relationships?

Establishing new patterns of beliefs and behaviors is always difficult. We seem to gravitate to the familiar even when it is uncomfortable. Giving ourselves permission to move into the uncharted waters of emotional independence and create new patterns for our lives takes courage and commitment.

Though it's often hard for us to give up the old habit of asking, "Mother (or Father, Husband, Boss, Child), may I?", we're living in an age when we have unprecedented opportunities to make our own decisions to be ourselves. As we embrace an expanded vision of ourselves and unravel our emotional dependencies, we learn that no one can fill us with confidence, independence, and a sense of inner worth but ourselves, with the help of whatever we interpret as our Higher Source.

Another very important piece of the courage-to-be-yourself puzzle is the awareness that the most essential and important connection we can make is with ourselves. We have heard this so often that we know it in our heads, but it is still difficult to believe it in our hearts and guts, because we have been socialized to conclude that our commitment is to others and our job is self-sacrifice. A pervasive underlying belief women grow up carrying is that they come last. Yet, without a deep commitment to and connection with ourselves, we cannot truly relate healthily to others.

Yearning to have my inner dependent and insecure feelings match my outer independent and successful demeanor, I began to search for ways to free myself from the tyranny of fear and learn how to express who I really was. It has been a great adventure—sometimes terrifying, often exciting, but always educational. Only since I began my quest to find Sue have I felt truly alive.

EMOTIONAL WISDOM

Women naturally possess an innate sense of connectedness—to God, to others, to our world, and to our own inner lives, which I call "emotional wisdom." Because of this wonderful emotional wisdom, we are relationship specialists. But too often we let our connection to our own inner lives languish and specialize only in keeping the peace in our outer relationships. True, their demands and needs can be loud and insistent, but our challenge is to give ourselves the same love and care we so readily lavish on others.

Being emotionally independent and connected to our authentic inner selves doesn't mean that we'll turn into selfish and self-centered women who are unavailable to others. It does mean that we're centered in an awareness of who we are— no longer fragmented by fear or unrealistic demands from ourselves or others. In reality, an emotionally independent woman is a happier, more loving and giving woman. As we find the freedom to express who we really, uniquely are, we tap into our inherent emotional wisdom and, as a result, create a climate around ourselves in which others can also grow, heal, and become better connected to themselves. Freed from the torment of looking outside ourselves for approval, and empowered by having our own identity, we have more to give. Plus, our lives are enhanced by a spirit of lightness and spontaneity.

Although *The Courage to Be Yourself* has no pat answers, it is filled with ideas and exercises designed to help you become aware of your fears, learn to transform them, move from emotional dependence to strength, and enhance self-esteem. Freed from the shackles of limiting fear, you can give yourself permission to own your own excellence and live up to your highest potential.

Even as we make progress, we may long to return to the easy fantasy that it's okay to be emotionally dependent, that others will take care of us, that it's their responsibility to keep us safe and support us. To *really know* that the buck stops with ourselves is frightening, but it's also extremely freeing to realize that we can be strong, independent, confident, and in control of ourselves. We are all—men and women—called to grow up and to assume responsibility for ourselves. As grown-ups we are better able to love—independently, interdependently, and joyfully.

We women are emotionally wise and wonderfully courageous. We have what it takes to overcome our fear-full inner dragons and live our lives expressing our true selves. I have been honored to walk with many women as they courageously tamed their dragons and surmounted obstacles and traumas that had once nearly destroyed their faith in themselves. As I said earlier, we teach what we need to learn the most, and that is certainly true in my case. So, as you read these pages, know that we are walking together. Live gently with yourself as you continue your journey toward being who you authentically are. Be patient with yourself, and please don't try to go it alone.

CHAPTER THREE

FACETS OF EMOTIONAL DEPENDENCE

A woman's public identity is her husband's
and her private identity, her children's.

VIRGINIA WOOLF

I was tempted to call this chapter, "Ya gotta name it to overcome it!" Why? Because we can only move beyond what is limiting or upsetting us when we honestly define what is going on. If we feel our identity is not our own, we must acknowledge that feeling before we can forge an identity for ourselves. If we've sacrificed our lives on the altar of everyone else's needs, we need to recognize the resultant malaise in order to remedy the situation. No matter what it is, we gotta name it before there is any hope that we'll learn to move around, over, and through it.

Toward that end, we will define some of the forms emotional dependence can take. Emotional dependence is many faceted and can put its depressive foot on our necks in a host of different ways. Anytime we come away from an encounter with someone feeling used or abused—not having stood up for ourselves or what we believed—it's a pretty sure bet we have acted, or not acted, out of an emotionally dependent internal space. When we find ourselves believing it's not okay for us to have a self who can come first—at least part of the time—when we know that our "self"-concept is really an "other"-concept, or when we suppress our feelings in order to please someone else, we have undoubtedly come face to face with a facet of our own emotional dependence. A profound and revealing question to ask ourselves during such times is "What was I afraid of that made me act this way?"

WHAT ARE LIMITS AND BOUNDARIES?

An emotionally strong and independent woman knows and states her limits. She can stay within the boundaries of what she knows is good for her in both her personal and public life. Because she gives herself permission to be herself, she is able to say no without guilt, or at least not let feelings of guilt keep her from doing what she knows is best for her health and well-being. Having emotional independence means we are no longer tied to the need for constant approval and are, therefore, not coerced into doing more than we feel comfortable doing by our need to please others.

Let's approach the idea of limits and boundaries through the backdoor. Do you ever allow people to treat you in a way that you secretly find unacceptable? For instance, do you try to keep the peace by quietly accepting unkind, disrespectful treatment that makes you feel devalued? I came from a family where teasing was a way of relating for some of the members. I hated it and felt hurt each time I was teased. I didn't ask for the teasing to stop because I feared that setting a limit would make them, especially my father, tease me all the more or (oh, horrors!) cause them to reject and ignore me. Finally, as an adult, I was able to tell the teasers that being teased was not acceptable to me. Without any fuss at all, they stopped. When we are really solid in our belief that we don't need to submit to unacceptable treatment, and state our limits clearly, it will probably stop.

Whenever we receive unacceptable treatment in silent suffering, or whine and beg ineffectually to be treated better, we ignore our limits and permit others to invade the boundaries of our self-respect.

When others need something, do they always call on "good old you" and know you will come through even if you've just come home from ten days in intensive care? Letting people take advantage of you is not honoring your limits.

If we say yes when we're actually yearning to say no, we aren't communicating our limits honestly, and we're setting ourselves up to feel resentful, hostile, and depressed. Women who do this tend to adopt one of two modus operandi: withdrawing from others or blowing their tops. Not being honest about our personal limits and boundaries creates feelings of betrayal, anger, defensiveness, and bewilderment, not only toward others but also toward ourselves. In our hearts we probably know that we've allowed fear to keep us from standing up for ourselves, so when we repeatedly allow our limits and boundaries to be trampled, we run the risk of lowering our self-esteem and losing respect for ourselves.

Learning to stand up for ourselves and honor our limits and boundaries involves, first, noticing when we're being taken advantage of; second, giving ourselves permission to have and to honor our limits and boundaries; and third, exploring and healing the fears that make us a living doormat. In order to stop giving ourselves away and have fair and open relationships with others, we must learn how to communicate our limits and boundaries honestly and effectively.

GIVING OURSELVES AWAY

Not respecting your limits and boundaries leads to giving yourself away, that is, putting what you want and need below the needs and desires of those around you. Among the people you know, including yourself, which ones get their wants and needs met most readily? Make an impromptu list of your acquaintances and their wants and needs, both tangible desires, such as a new car and a well-paying job, and intangibles, such as receiving respect, being heard, and having opinions valued. Are there any people on the list who always get what they ask for? Are there some persons who are more than likely to get what they want? Where do you rate by comparison? If you place yourself near the bottom, you're probably giving yourself away.

Maria lived for nineteen years with an emotionally abusive husband. She endured being put down privately and publicly and learned to "laugh it off." Having been raised a Catholic and holding staunch no-divorce views, she felt she had no choice but to accept her fate; thus, she gave herself away and came to loathe both herself and her husband.

We may give ourselves away in big chunks (not returning to school or work because it would inconvenience someone, or not speaking up when hurt or annoyed) or in small chunks (taking the brown banana). Eventually, both big and little chunks tossed aside result in living a life that is not our own. Please take a look at the following list of questions. If you can answer yes to any of them, you're probably giving yourself away to some degree:

1. Does fear limit your life?

2. Are you often filling the wants and needs of others without having your own needs met?

3. Do you say yes when you'd like to say no?

4. Are decisions difficult for you?

5. Are your close relationships unsatisfying?

6. Do you lack self-esteem and confidence?

7. Are you your own worst critic?

8. Are you overtired much of the time?

9. Does your life have little joy and spontaneous laughter?

10. Do you often swallow your opinions when they differ from others?

11. Do you regularly feel unloving and/or unlovable?

12. Do you wish your life were different?

Please don't be discouraged if you answered yes to one or more of the above questions. Most women probably would because we have been so thoroughly trained by society to deny our own lives. Thankfully we are eminently capable of *retraining* ourselves to adopt more loving and appropriate beliefs and behaviors. And that's what *The Courage to Be Yourself* is all about: *relearning* the art of being fully ourselves and, therefore, fully present to life and to those whom we care about. I wrote this book because I needed to unlearn what I'd been taught and give myself permission to stake a claim on my own life.

Women who give themselves away have a hard time making decisions because they're afraid of being wrong or appearing stupid if they make a mistake. When I separated from my former husband, I needed to buy a car. I looked at several but felt confused by the choices. I asked my estranged husband for his advice—an okay thing to do if asking as an equal, but I considered his opinion more valuable than my own. My intuition was screaming, "No, no, no!," but I ignored it and bought the car he chose.

That car and I were enemies from the very start. By not heeding my inner voice, I gave myself away—and got a car I could hardly live with. If I'd had the courage to move through my fear of making a mistake, heeded my inner voice, and made the decision for myself, I would have come away feeling better about my integrity—and probably have gotten a better car.

SAYING "YES" BUT FEELING "NO"

Ever come away from the phone after having said yes to making a zillion decorated cookies for a school party or working extra hours even though they conflicted with personal plans and you felt exhausted merely contemplating the task?

Afterward you dislike both yourself and the person to whom you said yes. Wishing you could turn back the clock, put steel in your spaghetti backbone, and firmly decline means you've just given yourself away.

Saying "yes" when we feel "no" probably means we've been "should-ing" on ourselves. We're afraid that we aren't being nice enough when we say no or that people will dislike us for letting them down. Yet I've discovered that when I'm convinced I have a right to say no and say it firmly, people accept it. They seem to get the message in direct proportion to how staunchly I hold the conviction. Replace draining "shoulds" with empowering words like *can, want to, choose to,* or *will.* For instance, "I *choose* to work late tonight" or "I *choose not* to work late today" is much more empowering than "I *should* work late" or "I *have* to work late tonight." "Shoulds" enslave us. "Choice" words help free and empower us.

A key method for having your "no" heard is to choose one statement and stick with it:

you:	I'm not able to chair this particular committee. I'm sorry.
they:	Oh, please! I don't have anyone else I can call.
you:	I know that's hard, but I'm not able to do it at this time of year.
they:	I don't know what I'll do. I'm desperate.
you:	It really is hard to organize this stuff, isn't it? I'm really sorry I'm not able to help you right now.

Notice that "You" stuck to the statement "I'm not able to," thereby honoring her limits and boundaries while expressing compassion for the other person's problem. "You" did not give herself away.

Before you say yes, take several deep breaths. Ask yourself if you are saying yes out of habit, guilt, or fear. Reassure yourself that you have the right to choose. Pause. Stop. If you feel unsure and need time to consider your alternatives, take it, and return the phone call later. You don't have to let yourself be terrorized by your own or other people's expectations of you.

THE TERROR OF EXPECTATIONS

Unrealistic expectations can cause us to give ourselves away to such an extent that we end up feeling we are a tiny little nubbin of exhaustion without one iota of energy left to do the next task. That may sound melodramatic, but haven't we all pushed ourselves past our limits because we felt we should do it all—and perfectly? Or because we felt others expected perfection of us?

Our own expectations and the expectations of others can kill us emotionally. All of us—women, men, and children, young and old—have suffered under the tyranny of expectations. Didn't we expect our honeymoons to be romantic and idyllic and our children perfect? Only a few are.

There's a scene in a play I once saw where one of the characters gives a wonderful commentary on expectations. She's talking to a classmate at a high-school reunion and says, "I thought that once he and I got together things would change. That's what's written over the women's entrance to Hell: 'Things Will Change.'"

Change is inevitable and to be expected, but so much of what we expect is sheer fantasy. We expect to be able to make our families happy. (Unfortunately, many of us have allowed our families, too, to expect us to make them happy.) We expect ourselves to be unfailingly bright, cheerful, and healthy. We expect ourselves to be unchangingly attractive, always patient and nurturing, a constant source of wisdom and comfort. Unrealistic expectations such as these are exhausting, not to mention terrifying and paralyzing.

One of the most crippling things we can do to ourselves is expect someone else to make us happy. Other people can only help to bring out what is already within us, such as the capacity to feel good about ourselves, to feel useful, to feel loved. When we feel unhappy and unfulfilled "because" of others, we can be sure we're giving ourselves away. We then need to take a long look at the beliefs and expectations we hold that are keeping us dependent on others.

Maria, the woman who was raised a Catholic and who was emotionally abused by her husband, finally said, "Enough!" To save her life emotionally, she left her husband. Unfortunately, because she took so long to free herself from the indoctrination of her church and to realize that she had other choices, her sons were old enough to resist leaving their school and home and chose to stay with their father. Had she honored her limits and boundaries sooner, maybe her marriage could have been salvaged and her mothering role secured. But so many years of swallowed pain and anger had created scars and animosity so deep that it was too late for the marriage.

It's important to notice that there's a definite difference between asking for what we want and need and expecting others to follow a hidden script we've written for them. Often, especially when strong-willed people are involved, there are going to be different ideas about how to live, work, and play. By adhering too rigidly to our interiorized picture of how things *should* be, we activate normal, healthy rebellion in other people.

My husband and I had a fairy-tale romance. We met in Hawaii and courted across the Pacific. It was perfect. We were perfect, confident that we'd been sprinkled with fairy dust and that our relationship would be forever blissful. Of course, it wasn't. After we'd settled into an everyday routine, our real lives began to get in the way of our expectations of happily ever after.

As a novice marriage counselor with a divorce in my background, I felt I had a pretty realistic picture of what my new marriage should be. However, my husband's wants, needs, and images differed significantly from mine. It took me a long time and a lot of grieving to realize that I was smothering our relationship with my expectations and my "expertise." I was activating my husband's rebel personality with my it-has-to-be-this-way script. After a great deal of inner struggling, I was able to stop terrorizing both of us with my idealistic expectations.

A funny thing then happened. After a cooling-off period, when he trusted that I had really gotten off his back, he began to inch toward being the way I'd earlier demanded that he be. Since I'd released those expectations and found other ways to fulfill my needs, his change was much appreciated (the chocolate chips in the cookie of life), but no longer necessary for my emotional survival.

As I found out, in even the most stable and caring relationships, there will be unmet expectations. I may expect a quiet evening of firelight and intimate sharing, and he may intend to watch basketball. We both may expect our kids for dinner, and they'll want to go have pizza with friends. We simply can't survive emotionally if we insist that every expectation be fulfilled. Life just isn't set up that way, so the healthiest response is to stay very flexible and not take it personally when our expectations fizzle.

THE HAVE-IT-ALL/DO-IT-ALL TRAP

One of the most damaging myths we've been led to believe is that we can have it all and do it all, in all ways, all the time. It's true, we can have it all on occasion and do it all for stretches at a time. We can even *be* it all for hours or days. But when we fall into the trap of trying to have, do, and be everything on a consistent basis, we run the risk of draining our energy reserves to a dangerous low.

One of my clients, Sarah, raised three children alone. Then she remarried and raised four more children—her stepson and three emotionally disturbed siblings whom she and her husband adopted. She made nearly all their clothes, cooked all the family meals from scratch, balanced a budget that would send chills up a contortionist's spine, and remained extremely active in her church. It upset her greatly when she occasionally felt unloving.

Sarah came from a background of trauma and deprivation that left her saturated with fear and struggling with deep emotional scars. Although she's one of the sweetest women I've ever known, fear of failure, abandonment, and not being lovable ruled her life. When she came to see me, she was desperately unhappy due to continually giving herself away, terrorizing herself with expectations only angels could live up to, and berating herself for a bewildering variety of real and imagined small inadequacies. To me, sainthood would have been appropriate for her, but she could only see herself through the lens of her abusive, neglectful, and frightening upbringing.

Little by little, with dedicated hard work, Sarah was able to fashion a small sign to hang over her soul, at least some of the time:

SUPERWOMAN DOESN'T LIVE HERE ANYMORE!

An important question to ask if we find we have chained ourselves to uncomfortable expectations is, "Who is defining what is meaningful to me?" Are you responding to your own or someone else's urgings? If you're following your own, are they kind and realistic nudges toward fulfillment or demanding kicks in the direction of perfection?

THE ART OF AVOIDANCE

When I was younger, I felt like an eager-to-please gerbil trapped on a wheel with no control over how fast it went. Now that I'm older and happier, life has settled into a more comfortable pace. But as I listen to the familiar ring in conversations among women who are compulsively juggling impossible tasks, obligations, and expectations, I feel exhausted. That was once me.

How and why did I allow myself to get so hopelessly trapped in the Have-It-All/Do-It-All syndrome? Two main reasons contributed to my frantic pace. First, my self-esteem had diminished to a record low and I was trying to convince myself that I was okay by doing a lot of different things and attempting to be wonderful and scintillating at all times. Second, I didn't feel I had what I wanted and needed, nor *was* what was wanted and needed to make life joyful and worthwhile. Busyness and overcommitment were my ways to avoid facing how unhappy I was with myself, my marriage, my parenting skills, my very life.

But avoidance doesn't work forever. Even though I had pretty much mastered the art, finally a very exhausted, depleted, weak, and vulnerable me had to acknowledge the truth about my unhappiness and the failure of my marriage. With a lot of help from friends and family, I slowly and laboriously found the courage to make several much needed changes.

What is your Have-It-All/Do-It-All trap baited with? Avoidance, guilt, and fear, as mine was? Please give yourself a life-saving gift and examine your motives if you are busier than you want to be. When we fear that we won't live up to others' expectations, and suffer guilt when we don't (or think we don't), we may be defining ourselves as a superwoman who can be everything to everyone. Such a definition pretty much guarantees that our expectations will rarely be met, and even when they are, we'll likely replace them with higher and ever-unattainable new ones.

Of course, women who are caught in the stranglehold of the Have-It-All/Do-It-All trap are often driven by economic necessity, as well as personal desire, to hold down a full-time job outside the home and a full-time job inside as well. Whether we're married or single, career women or at-home women, or both, we are often prodded mercilessly by an inner dragon to be perfect. As we find the courage to allow ourselves to be who we are—imperfect, but committed to growth—we begin to untie the ropes that bind us to emotional dependence.

Although we may embrace the paradigm of partnership and believe in our equality with deep conviction, it takes a great deal of courage and hard work to name and overcome the fears that block us from experiencing our emotional strength. As we learn to honor our limits and boundaries and free ourselves from the terror of unrealistic expectations, we will be well on the road to expressing who we authentically are.

CHAPTER FOUR

ALLOWING
OURSELVES
TO BE INVADED

My problem is that I forget what I know.

ESTHER HEFFRON JOHNSON

It's so important to break the pattern of looking outside ourselves for self-esteem. Asking others to mirror our value back to us inevitably leaves us feeling used and invaded. We also allow ourselves to be invaded if we constantly do for others and often resent that our own needs are not met; we doubt our decisions and beliefs and therefore acquiesce whenever someone disagrees; our children, mate, coworkers, and friends borrow from us without asking; we accept responsibility for other people's feelings and try to "fix" things; or people feel free to use our time thoughtlessly.

We become vulnerable to invasion through fear and lack of education: fear of rejection, imperfection, or confrontation and a lack of education about how to stand up for ourselves. Because we fear other people's reactions and don't know how to respond, we allow them to violate our limits and boundaries. Fortunately, our physical and emotional responses tell us when someone has trespassed on our private selves. We can learn how to tune into those feelings and use them as valuable clues for maintaining reasonable limits.

Invasion brings feelings of being taken advantage of, of having to give up something. If one of your children goes into your bathroom and borrows your hairbrush without asking, do you feel invaded, as if you've given up the right to have your things where and when you want them? If a hairbrush boundary has been clearly spelled out, the child has stepped past it, and you may well feel angry and resentful.

When you've just settled into a warm bath after a hard day at work and the kids bang on the door for you to settle a disagreement, whether you'll be invaded or not will depend upon your reaction. If, because of a false sense of responsibility for their happiness, you leap out of the tub and rush to solve their problems, you've allowed them to invade you. I know women who say they never have a moment to themselves because of the demands of their jobs and families. One woman told me she constantly feels as if she's being "nibbled to death by ducks."

Routinely doing for others what they are perfectly capable of doing for themselves invites invasion. Because doing too much has been an ingrained habit of mine for most of my adult life, especially with my kids, I was tickled with myself recently when I gave my adult son the name and number of a woman to call who has some medical referrals for him instead of making the call myself. A tiny triumph, one might think, but he had asked me to get the referrals for him and my knee-jerk reaction was to do so. Normally, calling her would be fine with me, but I am busier than my son is right now and probably would have felt resentful if I'd followed my habitual pattern of doing simply because asked.

In my mind I earn a gold star for honoring how I really felt and setting a limit. My son actually won also, because a resentful mother is neither a fun nor loving mother.

But it's not always outer circumstances that allow invasion and keep women going at a killing pace. Often invasion comes via requirements we impose on ourselves through adhering to the Have-It-All/Do-It-All syndrome. While it's true that the demands on a woman to play many roles are stressful, we do have the right to make choices that put ourselves first. In fact, regularly giving ourselves permission to be first may actually help others to grow as well. If we don't bound from the tub at first call, our children will need to rely on their own resources to solve their dispute. As we assert our independence, they will need to find their own.

FOOTPRINTS ON OUR FACES

When I was in high school, I gave my best friend, Jane, the nickname "Footprint" because she allowed her boyfriend to walk all over her. I'm sure I deserved the name, too, for the way I behaved with some of the boys I dated. My friend and I felt vaguely uncomfortable and powerless, but this was the 1950s and early '60s, when girls were encouraged to cater to boys. In many respects, times haven't changed all that much.

In lieu of honest and heartfelt talks with an adult, I remember reading as an early teen a series of little YWCA books on dating, menstruating, and the art of making a proper phone call. The booklet on dating actually said that in order to be popular (that summit of adolescent values), a girl should let the boy talk about himself. The booklet advised girls to ask the boy leading questions that would get him started talking about topics of interest to him. To build a boy's interest in me, I was to feign interest in cars and sports or whatever that particular boy liked.

Surely those books had been reprinted from volumes discovered in some moldy Victorian attic! I remember thinking, Isn't that a stupid game? What if there's a subject I'd like to talk about? My doubts manifested themselves in an interesting way: I developed a chronic frog in my throat. Especially when out on a date, I felt that I would choke at any minute. Often I'd need to excuse myself and find a private place to hack and cough. I was literally choking on the sincere words I held back and the game-like words I spoke. More basically, I was choking on the underlying message from those one sided, how-to-get-along-with-boys suggestions: You are not as important as they are. I carried that semi-hidden belief that I was second-rate with me into adulthood. I also carried my throat frog.

Several years ago I filled in an assertiveness inventory in a magazine. I was prepared to "pass" with flying colors because I had a master's degree in psychology and had been through a very growth-producing divorce. Feeling I'd made great progress in developing self-esteem, I was shocked and angered when I tested high in healthy assertion in all areas except in relationships with the men I loved, including my two sons.

The results of that test helped me discover that I was still acting out a lingering assumption that men are better, deserve to be listened to more than women, and would probably leave me if I didn't take a backseat to them in most matters. My beliefs allowed men to invade me by firmly planting their tennies on my face. Croak! Significantly, my need to clear my throat was a family joke and, I learned later, a constant irritation to my husband.

I decided to do something about both my beliefs and actions (or lack thereof). I began to assert myself with men, even with the men I loved. I ferreted out my fears and hidden attitudes of subservience and slowly stopped giving myself away. The process was not easy and required the help of a good therapist, supportive friends, clients, and my own stick-to-itiveness.

The frog in my throat, which had been with me constantly for almost thirty years, disappeared. Rarely do I choke and croak now, but if I do, I look for ways in which I've reverted to old patterns and allowed myself to be invaded. Froggie has become an important teacher.

THE PROJECTION PROBLEM

One of the most pervasive and destructive forms of invasion is "projection." Basically projection is a psychological term used for scape-goating. It's like a movie. The screen in front of us is blank until the images of the film are projected onto it. The film *uses* the screen to present its own pictures. The same principle holds true with people. If people are unable or unwilling to own their own internal feelings, they are likely to project them onto the blank screen of someone else.

For example, I need a lot of alone time and consider it a wonderful treat to have the house to myself. However, for many years both my husband and myself have worked at home, making home-alone-time very unpredictable. Because Gene is such a nice, easy-to-be-around guy, I felt ashamed of what I judgmentally saw as my "inordinate need" for solitude. That shame, as well as a fear of hurting him or making him angry, caused me to deny my feelings. Denied, the feelings multiplied like nuclear fission, and I projected them onto him and began to see him as inattentive to me. How nice. Now he was to blame and I was off the hook.

Sensing something was amiss among my mixed messages, Gene actually began to withdraw. That brought me up short and, as a result, I foraged around in my subconscious until I found the root of the problem—my own need for seclusion, which I had labeled unacceptable.

Projection is an uncomfortable defense mechanism for both projector and projectee. The person projected upon feels confused, helpless, defensive, and frustrated. On a conscious level, the person projecting his or her feelings onto others may feel righteous and blaming but underneath is actually vulnerable, fearful, and defended.

Projecting onto others those feelings we have disowned within ourselves means that our self-esteem and emotional strength are at a low ebb. Little self-esteem equals lots of blaming, shaming, and righteous externalizing. The greater our self-esteem and feelings of self-worth, the greater our ability to own our inner worms, darkness, and despair. When we act without consciousness or feel too vulnerable to be honest with ourselves, we will project onto others.

It's virtually impossible to change someone else's need to project, but we can fold up our screen and stop allowing ourselves to be projected upon. The most important thing to do about projection is to *recognize* it and not accept it as our own. I'll use another example of Gene and myself. One day I could tell he was upset, but he wouldn't tell me why. In answer to my prodding, he finally said, "I'm afraid I'll get in trouble if I tell you how I feel." Since punishing feelings is not something I do, it was easy for me to recognize this as a fear he was projecting from past relationships.

Some projections are not so easily spotted, but if you're feeling at your wits' end about a situation, a good question to ask yourself is, "Could this be a projection?" If the answer is yes, try to take it less personally, disengage, and gently and nondefensively call it as you see it. If you have difficulty knowing whether or not you're dealing with projection, as I often do, please give yourself the gift of finding someone to help you clarify.

Whether you are the recipient of projection, or engage in it yourself, which we all do on occasion, the best ways to fold up the screen are to shore up your self-esteem, reassure yourself, talk to friends, and learn the Anti-Projection Mantra: *Don't take it personally!* As they say in recovery programs, chances are "you didn't cause it, you can't change it, and you won't cure it."

ROLES TO CONQUER THE INVADER

One of the primary urges people need to fulfill in their lives is the desire to have and to express a personal sense of empowerment. Consequently, when we feel invaded or taken advantage of, we automatically seek ways to defeat the threatening invader. Until recently, society didn't encourage girls and women to develop their power. Naturally wanting and needing empowerment, we have gone underground and adopted secret and dishonest ways of having and using power. The trouble with such deviousness, though, is that in the long run, everyone who uses it loses.

Following are some of the secret and harmful strategies women have adopted as a defense against powerlessness and invasion.

MOTHER

There are only a few times in our lives when we need to be mothered. Some are early childhood, senility, illness, and emotional meltdown. The rest of the time, no matter who we are, we need to develop our own inner capacity to be strong and take care of ourselves. Yet women have chosen to mother men and other women, despite the thoroughly proven fact that an inappropriate and untimely mothering attitude means death to romantic love and the love between equal marriage partners, as well as to friendship.

I often find myself suggesting my women clients "monitor their momisms." A momism expresses itself in ways as trivial as telling a driver where to park: "Why don't you park by the bank?" You may say that this is just being helpful, but in the driver's mind it will most likely be interpreted as patronizing and as being unnecessarily controlling. The driver, consequently, is likely to feel he or she is being treated like a stupid, incapable child. No one enjoys being told that he or she can't perform simple tasks such as deciding where to park a car. Of course, if help is requested, that's different.

Another momism is nagging. When we feel the need to remind and reproach, we are nagging: "Have you done (___) yet?" "You shouldn't go out with only that light sweater! You'll catch your death of cold." "How many times do I have to tell you to do (whatever)?!" People soon learn to turn a deaf ear, or a rebellious back, to nagging.

To be fair, there's another side to the momism coin. Some men have a tendency to play "little boy" in an effort to get a woman to adopt the mother role, take care of them, and fulfill them inwardly. But you can stop your part. It may leave teeth marks on your tongue, but if you want to save your relationships with your mate, children, friends, and coworkers, stop being everybody's mom.

Momisms may seem empowering for a time but, in the long run, don't help you or anyone else. Momisms may, in fact, exhaust you and destroy your freedom and others' self-esteem. To the extent you feel the need to mother another adult, you will also shoulder his or her responsibility. If you are carrying all the responsibility in a relationship, why should the other person even attempt to carry his or her own? It's fascinating that the Chinese symbols for "attachment" and "mother" when combined mean "poison." When we attach ourselves to the role of mother, usurping others' right to learn from their own mistakes, we poison the relationship between us.

VICTIM

We all know people who play victim roles, people who go around sighing: "Poor me!" "If only they had…" "Whatever you want (sigh)." "I don't care (sigh)." "It's not important how I feel (sigh)." We learn these roles. We see our mothers and grandmothers manipulating others with them. But victims actually feel powerless and perceive themselves to be ruled by others' actions and judgments. However, the victim role is incredibly controlling because it evokes guilt.

People who play the victim role were often victimized in childhood, when they were helpless. As adults, they still feel powerless in their world. A perpetual victim never has to take responsibility for her or his own life because everything that happens is obviously and always someone else's fault. The victim personifies an emotionally dependent person because she's a captive of her reactions rather than the captain of her actions. Grown-up victims fill their lives with impossible "shoulds" and "have-tos," by which they dwell on their failures and beat themselves up continuously over their believed ineffectualness.

Alicia's father died when she was very young and she felt abandoned by him. Her mother was unstable and became more so after her husband's death. Being a "good" girl, Alicia took on the role of parent to her mother, and through the years preceding her mother's suicide, felt victimized by her situation. She had given up her childhood to her mother's emotional dependence. Alicia believed that no matter how much she loved, those she loved would leave her. She wanted and needed love herself, but, entrenched in the victim role, she had a series of relationships with men who either abandoned her emotionally or invaded every corner of her life.

Alicia needs to realize that she is responsible for casting herself in the role of victim. She is a "Yes, but..." person, so solidified in her identity as victim that she responds to every positive suggestion with "Yes, but..." followed by the reason why she can't be free of whatever person or situation is currently victimizing her. For instance, if I suggest that it might be good for her self-image, bank account, and marriage to get a different job, she says, "Yes, but there are no jobs" or "Yes, but I don't have up-to-date skills."

A victim puts herself and everyone with whom she relates in a can't-win position and in so doing calls forth frustration and pity, not the love for which she so desperately longs. In the depths of our beings, none of us really want that trade-off.

As women feel freer to express themselves, the victim role has taken an interesting twist. There are now deeply entrenched victims who act like righteous aggressors. They are likely to tell others how they should live their lives and argue vehemently with anyone who opposes them, defending their point of view loudly and often irrationally. The woman adopting this aggressive victim role is *always* right. If she feels hurt, it is *your* fault. If relationships become difficult, it is always the other guy who is wrong. If work is unsatisfactory, *they* are at fault. In an aggressive victim's life, everyone else is out of step but her.

Although their behavior is resoundingly different, under the surface, both weak and aggressive victims harbor very similar feelings. Each feels an overwhelming sense of inadequacy and is unwilling or unable to take responsibility for their own inner (and often, outer) lives. Whether they act helpless or righteous, victims are looking for someone else to fix their lives. Paradoxically, they often resist change no matter who offers it or how it is presented.

Regardless of how you express it, the only way to get out of the victim role is to *choose* to take personal responsibility for your life as it is now and as it can be. Accepting responsibility may very well require the guidance of a good therapist and/or honest friends who can lovingly help you understand how you use the victim role and its consequences in your life.

MARTYR

I once had a client who said, "Martyrdom is for emergencies only!" I love that statement for the depth of truth in it. We use martyrdom to get what we want from others, to bludgeon them into submission through guilt. When manipulating others, we martyrs can feel so chaste, noble, long-suffering, and self-righteous. But we can also feel incredibly lonely.

My grandmother was a grand mistress of martyrdom. No matter what anyone did for her, it wasn't enough. Experiencing continuous guilt around her caused the family to avoid her as much as possible.

No one feels comfortable listening while a martyr whines about all the ways we're responsible for her health, happiness, and self-esteem, and how we've all failed. By fostering guilt in others, the martyr contaminates herself and creates the very situation she fears: rejection, loss of love, isolation.

These thoughts and others like them are sure tip-offs that you're playing the martyr: "After all I've done for them!" "I gave him the best years of my life, and now look at what he's given me in return!" "If only the children would call once in a while."

Margaret, a class-A martyr, told me, "The children never call me (sigh)." (Both victims and martyrs sigh a lot.) When I asked if she ever called them, she replied that she didn't for fear they'd feel she was intruding.

Her kids were in a bind. They were supposed to read Mom's mind, and they were guilty if they didn't. Moreover, they'd spent a lifetime getting wise to her martyrdom, so they didn't particularly care to call her up for yet another load of guilt. Until she learned to take responsibility for conveying what she wanted and needed without punishing others with guilt, Margaret found herself alone a lot.

INVALID

There are individuals with physical challenges who are courageous beyond belief, who use their limitations to grow and stretch their intellectual and spiritual boundaries enormously, and, by the very way they handle pain, are inspirations to us. But the invalid I am referring to here is the woman who uses illness, real or imagined, to escape from life or to manipulate others. Who can invade us if we're always in ill health? No one can expect us to give much. No one can refuse to grant our needs and desires when we can't take care of ourselves.

Sonya was a picture of health while her five children were young and needed her constant care. However, as her kids began to grow up, branch out, and have lives of their own, she began to develop ill health. As each child prepared to leave home, Sonya's health failed more dramatically. Doctors were mystified because they could find no cause for her distress.

I met Sonya through her youngest child, Mattie, who had come to therapy to help assuage her guilt over leaving home and abandoning her "ill and helpless" mother. The three of us met together for several sessions in which Sonya, a very service-oriented person, courageously uncovered her unconscious belief that her life was as good as over when her mother role terminated its daily function. Her body was following her subconscious instructions and shutting down as each child left.

Sonya came to understand what she was doing and began to redefine her life by choosing different ways to serve. She learned more about her own unconscious process and is now a very healthy and active woman who provides a safe house for battered women and their children.

Sonya's invalid role was unconscious; Amelia's is not. Anytime Amelia's family tries to disagree with her, she has an asthma attack and retires to her bed where they can hear her gasping for breath because of what "they have said and done." In order to avoid the guilt of provoking attacks, her family eludes Amelia whenever possible.

Being chronically sick is powerful. True, little is expected of us, but look at the price we pay. When we're sick, our freedom is severely limited. Adopting the invalid role is in-valid!

XENA: WARRIOR PRINCESS

Totally opposite in appearance to the invalid is Xena: Warrior Princess. Unlike the victim or invalid, Xenas hold their swords high and declare defiantly, "Keep away—I can do it myself!" Xenas easily mistake attempts at friendship or intimacy as invasive and are immediately on the defensive. In fact, Xenas *expect* invasion and, therefore, see it even when it isn't there. Women may adopt the role of Xena if, early in life, they were either smothered with invasive, overprotective "love" or learned the difficult lesson that others could not be trusted to do or act as they promised. Too much unwanted attention as well as too little trustworthiness can lead us to believe we can only count on ourselves.

While Xena is a more empowered role to adopt than many others, it severs our connections with other people, leaving us strong but lonely and isolated. The Xena role is still a reaction to our own fear, not a proactive, free choice to be ourselves.

BITCH

> A man can be called ruthless if he bombs a
> country to oblivion. A woman can be called
> ruthless if she puts you on hold.

GLORIA STEINEM

Although some traditionally minded men (and women) will label us "bitch" if we're assertive and speak up for ourselves, that's best ignored. But some women deserve the derogatory title because they use bitchiness to relieve their pent-up frustration at giving themselves away and being invaded. They nag, gripe, use toxic humor, put people down, and criticize. And, secretly, they weep.

Being bitchy isn't much fun for the bitch or the bitchee. Bitchiness is generally the result of unspoken rage. It never works as a long-term solution because it corrodes self-esteem, alienates others, and cuts you off from your real self.

Adrienne used to nag her husband when he came home late, grumble about him to her friends, and gripe when he didn't do things he'd promised. When they came in for counseling, she was just as down on herself as on him.

They were locked in a deadly stalemate. She felt neglected and deserted, so she took on the role of bitch, admonishing and berating, explaining and raving, crying and raging. He played the role of martyr and penitent little boy—passively agreeing with everything she said, then aggressively doing exactly what he wanted.

Adrienne was willing to look at her underlying reasons for adopting the bitch role and to stop it, but her husband wouldn't give up his part of the game, and they eventually divorced. She's generally happy now, though she remembers her marriage with sadness. She's no longer bitchy, and she loves the experience of taking charge of her life. Her relationships are exciting and mutually supportive. Her husband has moved on, to a woman who's even more demanding of him than Adrienne was. Adrienne broke the pattern. He did not.

If you react to frustration by feeling like a powerless little terrier, snarling and ripping at a knotted sock, chances are you're playing the bitch. Find out what's frustrating you. How are you allowing yourself to be invaded? Do you feel you've given so much of yourself away that there's nothing left? Women who resort to bitchiness generally aren't really mean—they're scared, and they long for honest, complementary relationships.

GIRL-WOMAN

Women who play girl-woman are afraid too, but they take the opposite tack from the bitch. A girl-woman needs to be cared for and protected, fathered and told what to do. Somewhere along the way these women have made the assumption that they aren't lovable unless they're "less than." They may have received the idea that they're incapable of taking care of themselves from overprotective parents who didn't allow them to make decisions—including mistakes—and who taught them that if they wanted to get through life, they'd better find someone to take care of them.

Beth, a tiny, sweet woman, who was in one of our groups, talked in a soft little-girl voice and said that her husband didn't "let" her do many things. He wouldn't let her have a room in their house in which to paint, although he had both a study and hobby room of his own. She was very concerned that being in the group would make him angry. I said, "How old are you, Beth?" She replied, "Forty-six." After I asked her the question two more times, she looked up out of lowered eyes and giggled, "Sixteen." She had met her husband when she was sixteen, and there she had frozen, giving away her adulthood in order to hold his love, or so she believed. Subconsciously, she felt invaded, resentful, and depressed but was afraid that if she grew up, he wouldn't love her anymore.

Beth courageously challenged the role she had adopted and has changed dramatically. She speaks in an assured, adult manner, works as an administrator for a retirement facility, and is pursuing a graduate degree in gerontology, having designed the course of study herself. She's very happy with her husband. I asked her how old she was, and she replied proudly, "Forty-nine. And my husband likes me better this way!" As it turned out, her husband had felt burdened by her continuous need to be parented and he welcomed an equal relationship, though not without some initial resistance.

When you look inside yourself, do you find the uncomfortable and sabotaging feelings of mother, martyr, victim, invalid, Xena, bitch, or girl-woman? It can be scary to look honestly at our own behavior, but we can take comfort in the fact that virtually everyone who does it finds many things that need to be changed, and we all have the capacity to change ourselves for the better.

As we change, our relationships also begin to change. It is impossible for a relationship to remain the same when one of the persons involved alters his or her behavior. Facing the fear of change and acting in spite of it creates freedom. We can even use the greater fear of remaining in our painful ruts to impel ourselves into action. Frequently the other people in our lives are relieved when we give up negative roles and stop allowing ourselves to be invaded.

As the quote at the beginning of this chapter reminds us, we know! We just need to remember that we know. Remembering our true capabilities will assist us in finding the courage to be our brightest, most authentic selves.

CHAPTER FIVE

THE LEVELED LIFE

It is not the end of the physical body that should worry
us. Rather, our concern must be to live while we're alive—
to release our inner selves from the spiritual death that
comes with living behind a facade designed to conform
to external definitions of who and what we are.

ELISABETH KÜBLER-ROSS

Women who are emotionally dependent often carry an unspoken feeling that life is passing them by, that they have missed their personal boat somewhere along the way. Life, which had promised to be so exciting, full of joy and surprises, has turned out to be as level and barren as the salt flats. The truth is, if life feels flat, it probably means we're letting others define what our life should be and haven't taken the risk to find out who *we* are and what *we* want.

Children are natural-born risk takers. They move out into the world and toward others with their arms wide open. For children, life is full of mountains and valleys waiting to be explored. There's nothing level about the life of a healthy, spontaneous child. One moment she'll be rolling around in a fit of glee, and the next moment she's grabbing aggressively for her doll and sobbing.

When we see a child acting level and flat, we take her temperature. Why, then, do we feel it's okay for *us* to ooze through life on a boring, uniform plane? What, after all, is enthralling about a life that's safe but lacks wonder, enthusiasm, passion, and joy? What's normal about living from an apathetic place within ourselves that knows no spontaneous gratitude, sense of rightness, and harmony with the scheme of things?

Often we fall into the habit of living blah lives so gradually that we aren't aware of how flat and bland our lives have become. When my first husband left me, I realized how level my life was. When the shock wore off, I experienced an explosion of emotions. I'd be low, then I'd skyrocket into a frenzy of rage and desire for revenge. I'd be thinking of suicide, then I'd be giddy with fantasies about the possibilities that lay open before me.

During the years it took to heal those wounds, I experienced the widest range of feelings that I'd had since I was a teenager. Becoming aware of how painful my life was because of its flatness, I decided to do something about it. One of my first, fleeting reactions was, "I'm never going to let myself be hurt like this again. Never, never, never!" To protect myself, I locked myself up in an emotional bubble-dome, out of reach and invulnerable. But that didn't last long because I gradually began to understand my own role in the breakup: how my emotional dependence and low self-esteem had helped level my life.

During my first marriage, I was unwilling to be aware of what was going on inside of me or in the relationship, for that matter. It was simply too scary. As a defense mechanism, I became funny on the outside, covertly and ineffectually venting my anger by telling funny but barbed stories. Later, when I was able to see my actions with love and forgiveness instead of flinching, I chose to act differently. I changed my promise never to be hurt again to two affirmations that I still live by.

The first was *I choose to live my life fully.* For me, that meant a commitment to risk taking and to experiencing *all* of my feelings, whether joyous, painful, or indifferent. It also meant a commitment to honor dreams long shelved. I had tried to avoid pain and risk for years. Now I was learning that in order to live *my* life I had to embrace life's whole package: the pain as well as the joy, the risks as well as the certainties—the entire gamut of emotions and possibilities. It wasn't a decision I made lightly or easily.

I was helped immensely by this passage from Kahil Gibran's *The Prophet*:

> *Your joy is your sorrow unmasked*
> *And the selfsame well from which your laughter rises*
> *   was oftentimes filled with your tears*
> *And how else can it be?*
> *The deeper that sorrow carves into your being,*
> *the more joy you can contain.*

My second affirmation was *I will never give myself away again.* Giving myself away had depleted me so much I no longer felt there was a "me." To counteract that void, I decided to explore my boundaries, beliefs, and desires. What did I want to do with my life? Whom did I want to do it with? What behavior was acceptable to me? What could I do to increase my independence and my ability to love others? How could I be a supportive yet firm parent? What dreams longed to be fulfilled? What did I need to heal in order to resist the temptation to give myself away again?

As a result of my inner exploration, I finalized the divorce, went to graduate school, and learned to become a better parent and friend to myself.

RESISTANCE MAGNIFIES PAIN

That the yielding conquers the resistant and
the soft conquers the hard is a fact known
by all persons, yet utilized by none.

LAO TZU

Natural childbirth classes teach mothers-to-be that the pain of childbirth is greater when you resist it and grow tense with fear. They tell you to "breathe into the pain," not because deep breathing decreases the pain, but because relaxation increases your ability to accept pain.

In my bereavement groups I meet many people who try to resist their pain. I encourage them to turn toward it, relax into the experience of pain, give themselves permission to feel it and act on it. This frequently amazes them because most have been taught the stiff-upper-lip approach to both physical and emotional pain.

Resistance magnifies pain. The more we resist difficult people, concepts, or circumstances, the more we draw to us exactly what we're trying to resist. Perhaps that's what Jesus meant when he spoke of turning the other cheek. Resistance causes tension. Tension creates tightness, stiffness, and inflexibility. And being stiff, tight, and inflexible makes us vulnerable. In a windstorm, the heavy oak tree resists and the willow yields. The willow, which allows the wind to whip through its branches, clearly has the better chance of surviving.

Remember this formula:

RESISTANCE → TENSION → INFLEXIBILITY → VULNERABILITY

When you feel the first sign of resistance tension, become aware of who or what you're resisting. What circumstances, memories, attitudes, or relationships are threatening you with pain? Are you magnifying the pain by resisting it?

Acknowledge what you discover about your patterns of resistance. Then accept that a source of pain exists and you are feeling resistant toward it. Finally, choose to let the pain be present and to act appropriately. Resistance is habitual reaction, not free choice. Freedom is created by your ability to choose how you want to act and react.

Resistance can also signal the presence of a power struggle: a desire to be right, to prove a point, to be in control. The only way to win a power struggle is to give it up. Resistance to other people's opinions and feelings is just as useless as resistance to our own. Our pain or discomfort is magnified in direct proportion to our resistance. When loved ones are cranky and we think they shouldn't be and we resist their mood, we'll feel worse and very likely provoke them further. However, we don't have to stick around and bear the brunt of their mood. Only they can change it, so resistance is futile.

Sylvia hated her husband's constant put-downs about her weight and the fact that he rarely told her he loved her. She entered into the spirit of the power struggle, pointing out every small action and comment that proved that he was wrong and unloving. In her resistant mood, she couldn't see or absorb any of the loving things he did do. They became like two boxers, jabbing the air in their respective corners in anticipation of the next round. Both were in pain.

As she became aware of the destructive path they were taking, Sylvia gradually stopped resisting. She didn't give up her rights, but she quit nagging and judging her husband. She became more flexible and was able to express her real feelings instead of lashing out in revenge. She stated her wants and needs, but not in an accusing, critical way. When he couldn't give her what she needed, she became creative at filling her own needs. She stopped resisting him and chose instead to make a better life for herself, not out of resentment toward him but out of love for herself.

As Sylvia gained independence, she began to feel less like her husband's victim and more able to reach out to him with love. He'd been resisting her demands for love and affection, but as she demanded less, he felt more like giving.

THE HIGHER YOU GO, THE FARTHER YOU'LL FALL

Many of us believe that life is like a pie. It's dished out in large and small pieces and when it's gone, it's gone. Therefore, we don't tempt the gods by asking for too much. After all, if we ask for more than our share, we're just begging to be disappointed. We've probably been trained to believe that the higher you go, the farther you'll fall.

When we were children, and the joy of risking and stretching was still natural to us, we were warned:

- Don't get too excited.
- Remember, there are only two spots on the cheerleading squad, and fourteen girls trying out for them.
- Don't get your heart set on it.
- You'll cry as hard tomorrow as you laughed today.
- Don't expect too much from (____). ("Marriage" is a good fill-in for this one.)
- Life is hard.
- Don't rock the boat.

What are the underlying messages behind such statements? Maybe some of these:

- It's dangerous to risk.
- It's dangerous to hope, to be happy, to expect life to be good and fulfilling.
- There's not enough to go around.
- Give up your childlike awe and wonder.
- Enthusiasm inevitably leads to disappointment.

I know a woman whose favorite statement is "Life is hard and then you die." What's your image of a woman whose life is determined by such a statement? Is she constantly threatened by scarcity? Yes. Does she cling to the old because risk taking is scary? Yes. This woman believes that life is hard. Guess what? For her, it jolly well is. She gets what she believes life will give her.

If you're one of the older children in your family, can you remember the birth of your first younger sibling? I do. I remember being both excited and scared. Would my parents have enough love for both of us? They assured me they would, so I began to look forward to *my* baby. Then my grandmother gave me this input, which was all too easy for seven-year-old to take to heart: "Even though your mother and father will now have someone they love more than you, I'll still love you." You can imagine how I welcomed my baby sister after that—with open hostility. Because I believed I'd be unloved, I felt unloved. I *was* loved, but for many crucial years I was unable to feel it. And this scarcity of feeling loved contributed much toward the leveling of my life in adulthood. It was only with the patient help of friends, my mother, and therapy that I was eventually healed.

The leveling message Linda received from her family was that she must "do it right or don't do it at all!" She was never given permission to learn, risk, and experiment, so she developed a pattern she called "slip 'n' quit." Since only angels always do things right the first time, and since she had never been encouraged to make mistakes and therefore had no support system to buoy her up while her life jacket was in for repairs, she took up a whole series of things in which she slipped and quit, including ice skating and ballet.

Linda was afraid to climb higher for fear of falling farther. Her habit of slipping and quitting fostered a fear of trying, so she settled for less and less, shedding dreams almost before she was fully conscious of them. Her life became monotonous and monotone.

Linda's story has a happy ending. As she became aware of her limiting pattern, she was able to give herself permission to try new things even if she did them wrong. Linda is becoming a loving parent to herself and is gradually acquiring more and more courage to be who she really is. Giving herself a much needed infusion of enthusiasm, she has risked taking a new job and is loving it. With her change in attitude, other areas of her life are also being suffused with fresh energy. She told me she still slipped, but that she had been able to keep her promise not to quit.

SAFE BUT SORRY

When we settle for less in order to feel safe, we always feel sorry. If we compromise our dreams, limiting ourselves with negative ideas gleaned in childhood or adulthood; if we accept that it's useless to ask for what we want and need; if we believe lack is safer than abundance, our lives will close around us like a safe but suffocating blanket.

We do need security, but security can be purchased at too high a price. Security obtained at the expense of exhilarating, creative growth and change merely strangles us. Surely the caterpillar feels secure in its cocoon but when it emerges, it needs to unfold its wings and risk flight.

Give up your need to be safe but sorry. Resolve your grief over the leveling of your life by choosing to unfold your wings and take flight. Have the courage to SOAR: Stretch Out And Risk. You *can* do it.

SELLING YOUR DREAMS SHORT

There are few greater disappointments than realizing our lives have been a series of compromises that have caused us to sell our dreams short. Selling our dreams short is selling ourselves short and setting the stage for regrets, "what ifs," and "if onlys."

As a hospice volunteer I am privileged to be with people at the end of their lives. As you might imagine, the fewer regrets a person has, the more readily they meet death with courage, grace, humor, and equanimity. However, when patients feel they have not lived the life their personal dreams indicated, the path to death's door is strewn with regrets.

You don't need to let that happen to you. It's never too late to recall your dreams and pursue them enthusiastically. If you have lost touch with your dreams and desires, a good way to retrieve them is to remember what you dreamed of doing and being as a kid. I wanted to be an actress. As a little girl, I would play out the parts I'd seen in movies. My favorite reenactment was being Tarzan and swinging from tree to tree (leaping from bed to bed when my parents weren't home), lugging Jane (my pillow), and bellowing a blood-curdling yell.

Although I acted in plays in high school and college, for the most part during my first marriage and the first few years of this marriage, I squashed the acting bug because it inconvenienced my family. But the bug refused to die and my resentment definitely flourished, so I gathered up my courage and went back to acting when I was forty. For ten wonderful years, I thoroughly enjoyed being part of an excellent community theater group. After that, I was honestly satiated and could say, "Been there, done that."

Another dream that will not die is Jill's dream of motherhood. Since she was six years old, Jill has wanted to get married and be a mommy. But fate can be fickle and uncooperative at times and, at thirty-eight, Jill is an unmarried career woman whose desire for marriage and a family has not abated. Although she realizes that single parenthood will not be easy, Jill also feels she is meant to be a mother and that her life will not feel complete without a child. After much thought, Jill has decided to fulfill the part of her dream that she can and is in the process of adopting an infant. I admire her courage and determination not to sell her dream short.

What did you dream of when you were a little girl and an early teen? What do you love to do now? What do people tell you your talents are? What makes you feel whole and happy when you do it? Discovering the answers to these questions can help you find and follow your dreams.

We experience cycles of passionate interest during our lifetime and dreams may change as a result. But, no matter how they appear, dreams remain an integral part of who we are. If we slay persistent dreams on the altar of practicality or other people's desires, we sacrifice a crucial part of our creative self that yearns for expression. The price is too high when we sell our dreams short. Please start making yours a reality while you are still able.

When I was young and feeling low, my dad used to tell me, "It's just one of those little valleys on the highway of life." I didn't much appreciate the statement then, but I've since come to understand how right he was. If we are to enjoy the "high ways" of life, we need to find the courage to Stretch Out And Risk by experiencing the valleys as well.

CHAPTER SIX

GETTING THERE: A ROAD MAP

We're not yet where we're going but
we're not still where we were.

NATASHA JOSEFOWITZ

Are you sitting beside your life's road waiting for someone to come along and give you a ride? Someone to take you on *their* trip? When I was growing up, women were taught to wait patiently for life. Some of our best tour guides were Doris Day and Rock Hudson, Ozzy and Harriet Nelson, TV programs such as *Father Knows Best*—and our own mothers.

Thankfully this form of brainwashing has changed dramatically and young women now have stronger, more self-reliant role models. However, external change is often in place for quite some time before it is internalized in a majority of women. Although no longer shackled to where we were, emotionally we are not yet where we are going. Our journey is toward an unshakable belief in our worth and wisdom and the invincible courage to be who we were born to be. We are moving in that direction, a feat we can be proud of.

Who ever heard of a damsel rescuing a knight in distress? We may do it all the time, but we were taught to act as if someone else were in the driver's seat of our life. It doesn't work! The adventure is our own. We need to chart our own course and make our own decisions in order to be true to who we really are.

No matter where we're going—to the supermarket, to work, to Europe, to a career, to marriage—we need maps to show us how to reach our destination. We also need road maps for our trek toward higher self-esteem and greater emotional strength. This book is designed to provide you with many maps that have helped me, my clients, and friends find our way to greater inner freedom. I encourage you to use these maps gently and tolerantly.

Road maps generally contain a large, overall map, plus smaller maps of the cities in the area. The "big map" I want to share with you is:

THE THREE-A MAP

AWARENESS: Become *aware* of your feelings. Inner awareness is the beginning of outer change.

ACKNOWLEDGMENT: *Tell* a trusted friend or counselor about your awareness.

ACCEPTANCE: *Honor* where you are and what you are feeling. Be gentle with yourself. You are okay just as you are, even as you seek to change.

The first and most basic step for any change or growth, no matter how small, is to know what we feel, how we think, and how we would like to alter our lives. In other words, we need to be *aware* of where we are and where we want to go. It's then important to *acknowledge* where we are to someone else. Acknowledgment keeps us honest and helps us break out of denial. When we realistically acknowledge what we have become aware of to ourselves and to a trusted friend, we are more likely to move forward. Finally, *acceptance* alleviates shame and guilt and helps propel us out of limiting patterns while energizing us for needed change.

Let's look at these three steps in more detail.

AWARENESS

All change begins with awareness. Becoming aware of what we're thinking and, even more important, what we're feeling, enables us to work with and change our attitudes and actions. When we're not aware of what we're feeling, the feeling becomes our master. Suppressing or repressing an emotion causes us to lose control over how we express it, and express it we will. A repressed or suppressed emotion builds up power until it's impossible to contain and, as a result, erupts destructively. Being aware of our feelings before they become hard to control allows us to choose how to express them constructively.

Being aware of our feelings sounds easy, but it's not because many of us spend our entire lives pushing feelings aside as we try to please others. Our wants and needs may be lost in the process. Consider this poem by Anne, a career woman with two children, a husband, and a difficult live-in father-in-law:

Saturday

The family has gone on an outing,
Responsibilities I've put on the shelf.
This Saturday I have been counting
On spending some time on myself.

But life is full of vexation.
That fact should have given me a clue
To expect unexpected complications
...I've forgotten what I like to do!

Anne had lost herself while constantly attempting to please others. Depression was a daily battle because she had repressed her own, unfulfilled needs. When she began to see that she, too, had rights, that she was not required to sacrifice her life to her family and her job, she also became aware of what she wanted and needed. In therapy she began to detach herself from the old, burdening sense of responsibility for the lives of everyone around her. Now that she is making a life for herself, her depression has lifted. Interesting, Anne also feels more loving toward her family.

A word of caution: As you begin to honor your feelings and needs, you may find others labeling you as selfish, or you may find yourself *feeling* selfish. Because most of us were taught to think of others first, we may initially feel strange and even self-indulgent when we stop denying our own feelings, wants, and needs. Remembering that suppressing needs and desires causes more harm to ourselves and our loved ones than being aware of them does helps us have the courage to identify our feelings.

Another obstacle to greater awareness is the fact that lack of awareness pays off in short-term ways by letting us ignore pain and anger. When Ruth was a child, her mother beat her when she misbehaved or spoke out of turn. Ruth learned to turn off emotionally, to detach herself from people, avoid intimate relationships, and become virtually invisible. As a child, those were survival skills; as an adult, they were severe limitations.

Ruth became so good at detaching herself from her feelings that she actually did not feel the pain of those beatings. Today the little girl inside her, whom she still tries desperately to protect, is afraid to get too close to people. As a result, Ruth feels isolated and lonely. What helped her survive in the past keeps her separated in the present.

Many of the choices we made when we were young were wise at the time. As we learn to deal with our fears in new and more creative ways, it's crucial that we be very patient and gentle with ourselves. It's not at all appropriate to feel guilty for childhood patterns that may have helped us survive. After all, when we made those early decisions, we were doing the very best we could. And, in many cases, our decisions were truly heroic.

Now, however, as adults, we can make it safe to honestly think and feel what is ours to know and experience. Simply being aware that "Hey, I don't like it when she says that to me" can be very liberating emotionally. Freedom starts with knowing how we feel.

Awareness begins with an inner inquiry that goes something like this: What am I feeling? When did it start? Where does my body hold it in the form of anxiety or tension? Is it a familiar feeling? How is this feeling limiting me? What am I afraid might happen?

Inner dialogue helps us stop blaming circumstances and other people for the hurts and disappointments in our lives. It allows us to assume responsibility for our own reactions. As we talk things through with ourselves, we'll become more and more able to sit in the driver's seat of our lives.

The key to emotional strength and personal freedom is always to bring the responsibility back to ourselves. We may not be able to change events, but we can change our response to them by asking, What am I doing? Why? Why am I saying this? How am I setting this situation up?

To be effective, the dialogue must be conducted with kindness and respect. If you blame and verbally abuse yourself for problems and situations, you'll drown yourself in guilt, which will keep you from healing and transforming uncomfortable feelings. Don't use responsibility as an excuse for beating yourself up emotionally. If you start to feel guilty, ask yourself who is demanding that you feel badly. You'll probably run across an internalized critical-judge voice.

Frequently, when we use inner dialogue, the person we're talking with is our inner, vulnerable child. If we're not careful to be understanding and tolerant, our inner child will hide, and we won't be able to understand the choices she's making that cause us to be weak and vulnerable.

Becoming aware of feelings is like shining a light in the closet to make sure all the bogeymen and goblins will run away. You may think, Well, it's easy for you to talk about inner dialogue, but I've got so much junk buried inside that if I open the door, it'll completely overwhelm me. Fear of being overwhelmed can keep you stuck in very painful patterns. Hopefully, as you read on, you will gain some insights and practical tools for dealing with your fears in manageable, bite-size chunks.

In my work with women, I've discovered that we seem to have an inner-control mechanism that doles out just as many slimy toads and beasties as we can handle at any given time. The fear of being overwhelmed is a huge hinderance when it encourages us to *under*whelm ourselves and avoid facing our difficult feelings.

If you sense that you have hidden fears that threaten to spew out with volcanic force, by all means see a therapist immediately before you begin to work on your own. Some people have repressed fears that can only be healed with compassionate and competent professional help.

While many of us will need strong, objective, professional hands to hold at times, more often than not we can parcel out our inner discoveries by ourselves or with the help of friends.

ACKNOWLEDGMENT

The next step toward change is acting on our awareness. Fully acknowledging a newfound realization helps us reconnect with others. Fearful secrets separate us from people. Secrets are like mushrooms: put them in a dark place, cover liberally with manure, and they will "mushroom."

Honestly and gently acknowledging our feelings and beliefs breaks the isolation and loneliness in which we live. Of course, it is essential that we share our secrets only with those who will honor them and our process. First and foremost, we need to be able to trust that *we* will handle our own inner discoveries carefully, even reverently. We all need to feel understood and connected to ourselves and to others. In a climate of nonjudgmental love, we can truly become who we are meant to be.

There are many styles of acknowledging. My own style is to talk openly and honestly about my fears and the dark, nasty feelings I have inside of me. I process my feelings more quickly and efficiently when I verbalize them. If my feelings are out in the open, verbally hanging in the atmosphere, I can sort through them in order to understand and change them. Without the understanding of others, it takes me much longer to process my feelings. When understanding ears are scarce, I use my journal to talk to myself.

My internal process works best when it's externalized. Unexpressed, my feelings grab me by the neck and strangle me. It has been absolutely essential for me, in developing the courage to be myself, to find people who will hear me without judgment and who will know with me that "this, too, shall pass." I sort as I talk, but other people have different methods. For example, in explaining her way of processing feelings, one of my dearest friends says, "I have to crawl under the couch with the dust bunnies in order to make sense of my own grubby attic and moldy basement."

Become aware of the ways in which you most naturally and comfortably acknowledge. What helps you move toward being really you? Is writing down how you feel helpful? Does talking to yourself in the car help clarify things? Do you need to be heard by another? Be flexible. Allow yourself to experiment with what works and what doesn't. Develop a style that is right for you. Styles may change as we evolve. Mine certainly has. I can now benefit from processing feelings quietly and internally, which wasn't true a few years ago.

As you hone your skills of awareness, at some point, it will be important to acknowledge to someone other than yourself. Doing so helps reinforce your awareness. Also, experiencing the acceptance of another human being supports your own self-acceptance.

Too often, we create limiting feelings by speaking to ourselves in a judgmental, no-win voice, saying such things as, you should; you must; you shouldn't. These words activate internal responses such as, I won't! I can't! To resolve this kind of internal civil war, use words such as *could, choose to, want to, can, will,* and *will not.* This may seem like an overly simplistic technique, but it's not. Words similar to *should* and *have to* imply that we are powerless to choose. *Will* and *choose to* let us know we are free to make conscious choices.

Have you ever said, "I feel sad," only to have someone retort sternly, "You shouldn't feel that way!" It stopped the conversation, didn't it? The connection with the other person was broken. Choose well the persons with whom you share your innermost feelings. You have a right to have your feelings, whatever they are, and painful feelings can be transformed, transmuted, and healed only in a safe, accepting environment.

Learn to be a trusted friend to yourself, and find friends and therapists who are trustworthy. Use your intuition in making these choices. You can only be honest in exploring your feelings if you don't fear the response from either yourself or others.

When we're told we "shouldn't" feel sad or lonely or whatever, we will hesitate to open up again. And wisely so! We need and deserve to be treated with tenderness, respect, and understanding. As we heal and grow, it is best for us to reveal ourselves only to those who can accept our acknowledgment gently. Talking to a trusted friend about our real and imagined shortcomings and struggles to improve helps us learn to forgive ourselves.

ACCEPTANCE

> Do your best, even if you make apparent mistakes. How are you to judge if they are mistakes? You can only obey the higher urge which inclines you to contribute the best that you have to the service of the community of [humans] and angels. Thus, you shall be an ever growing channel for the light.
>
> WHITE EAGLE

The third part of the road map is acceptance. After you become aware of feelings and thoughts and acknowledge them, you need to accept them in order to move through them and transform them.

Remember, feelings are neither right nor wrong—they just *are.* When you can accept your feelings, you'll be able to risk being outwardly honest. If you criticize and judge yourself for your feelings, you'll close down, hide, and relate less honestly to both yourself and others.

Who likes to be browbeaten? How many times have you said, "I know it's so stupid, but I feel…" or "I know it's awful, but I feel like…" or "Oh, you dummy! How stupid can you be?" If our feelings are always greeted by this kind of unloving, condemning diatribe, is it any wonder we don't want to express them, even to ourselves?

We can free ourselves from old rules about right and wrong and from judgmental self-talk. My own self-talk used to be excruciating. For instance, if I didn't like someone, I'd berate myself with such wonderful put-downs as, "Who are you not to like her? You're not so swift yourself!" or, "You are only really a nice person if you love everyone."

Now when I have such feelings, I look at them closely, check to see if that person is mirroring something to me that I dislike about myself, confide in a friend if possible, and then give myself permission to feel the way I do.

Accepting our feelings as they are provides an inner climate that's conducive to growth and change. Safe in the arms of acceptance, we no longer need to pretend. We can speak out and bring secrets into the open to be healed. Acceptance nurtures, and nurturing allows us to flower into the beautiful blossoms we are meant to be.

Honoring where you are and what you're feeling allows you to choose to move on to something different if you want. Give yourself a break. You're okay, and you're on the road to being even more okay.

Accepting yourself as you are is an act of forgiveness toward yourself. Forgiving yourself makes it easier to forgive and accept others.

An excellent way to foster forgiveness and acceptance is visualization. Think about something you dislike about yourself or something you wish you hadn't done. Say to yourself, "I did the best I knew how at the time; I am now willing to forgive myself." Visualize yourself putting whatever you regret into a basket attached to a beautiful helium balloon. Now take a deep breath and watch the balloon and basket float away. Bless it as it goes. Throughout your day, repeat the visualization. Tell yourself that you are now willing to release guilt and forgive yourself, but don't expect to have instant feelings of absolution. Negative emotions harbored within for long periods take time to be cleansed. As you gently and patiently persist, your feelings will change.

Julie's story exemplifies the power of the Three-A Map. Julie's mother was critical and abusive. In her therapy sessions with me, Julie *became aware* that she was trying to give me all the right answers, in order to avoid any possibility of my criticizing and judging her. She was trying too hard to please me, a mother figure, and be accepted by me. Later, she *acknowledged* this awareness to a personal friend, and they both *accepted* it without judgment.

In her next session with me, Julie spoke from such an honest place within herself, and it felt so completely natural to her, that she simply forgot to tell me about her mother-insight. At the end of our session, she realized that she was no longer trying to please me by saying all the right things. She then told me how using the Three-A Map had freed her from her initial fear of me.

As Julie's story shows, sometimes all it takes to change a behavior pattern is to *see* it and *say* it.

ALTERING COURSE

The Three-A Map of awareness, acknowledgment, and acceptance is a practical tool for transformation. Using it helps you discover the course you wish your life to take and allows you to uncover the strengths that will guide you on your way. Each of the Three A's is important, but please know that acceptance is absolutely essential. Only after you've accepted your truth can you move onward to alter that which is limiting your freedom. Changing patterns that no longer work for you will change your reality. And when your reality reflects your real self, you will be on the perfect, right course for you, and experience the sensation of authenticity that we all crave.

Being yourself is your birthright. You have all the tools within you to enable you to express yourself and your potential without being limited by fear.

PART TWO

Facing the Dragons in the Dungeon

CHAPTER SEVEN

FEAR! OUR GREATEST OBSTACLE

Though no one can go back and make a
brand new start, my friend, anyone can start
from now and make a brand new end.

ANONYMOUS

One of the hardest things I ever needed to face was the extent to which fear ruled my life. As I explored my own limiting fears, I discovered that I wasn't alone in my fear of emotional independence. Many women harbor a secret fear that they don't have what it takes to be in charge of their lives and responsible for their choices. In order to be liberated from patterns of behavior that limit our self-expression, happiness, and ability to truly love, we must find the courage to face the dragons in the dungeon—the furtive fears that flourish deep within our psyches.

NATURAL AND LEARNED FEARS

We are naturally curious, not naturally fearful. A baby is born with only two natural fears: fear of falling and fear of loud noises. When a baby is about to fall or hears a loud noise, it immediately goes into a fear response, inhaling sharply and stiffening. The infant's initial physical reaction is followed by panicked crying. As adults, we still experience these primal, natural fears. All other fears, including fear of death, are learned.

Our culture, families, churches, and governments use fear to control us. Used sparingly, fear can be a useful means of instruction. But all too often it's applied inappropriately, and we're conditioned to unhealthy fearfulness. We come out of childhood wearing the yoke of our family's and society's unresolved anxieties such as the fear of failure, embarrassment, death, appearing ignorant, and not being as good as the Joneses. Conditioning causes us to adopt other people's fears as our own.

My mother was deathly afraid of dogs. She never expressly told me to fear dogs, but as a child my sensitive mind registered her fear response whenever a dog appeared. I learned that dogs were dangerous. Even though I'd never been bitten and had known only one person who was bitten, my body reacted with a fear response whenever I saw a strange dog. As a young adult, I realized the origin of the fear and worked through it.

The good news about learned fear is that it can be unlearned. It is possible for us to release ourselves from the grasp of borrowed fears and overcome ones that are ours alone. Unlearning fear takes a strong desire to be free and a willingness to patiently retrain ourselves. In our era of cell phones, split-second computers, and fast food, we have come to expect instant gratification. But a fear-free life doesn't happen magically or instantaneously. Self-discovery and growth are elements of an ongoing process of evolution. Yes, there will be sudden, breathtaking insights, but without patient effort and commitment to the day-to-day work of change, they will quickly fade.

I have been working on my tenacious fear of rejection for thirty years. When I first began, patience was by no means my strong suit, and there were times when I felt discouraged to the point of despair. Sometimes I still backslide or creep forward way too slowly for my taste, but I can truly say that now my fear of rejection is only a tiny thread, a fragile web slightly restricting my life, whereas when first discovered, it was a heavy chain and anchor.

Of course fear may also be learned as a result of traumatic experiences. Many women fear men because they have been raped, molested, or otherwise physically or emotionally abused. If something frightening has happened to you, you will probably need the help of a minister, therapist, or other trained professional to help in uncovering and healing your inner wounds.

No matter what our past, we can relearn our fundamental attitudes toward life and also experience the deep truth that our life and relationships need not be fear-filled. We are not our fear; we simply experience it. Step by step we can internalize the reality that fear is not something we *are* but something we *have*. For example, you may have told yourself, I'm such a wimp. Not true. Never accept a definition of yourself that identifies you as your fear. You may feel fearful, but that doesn't mean you're a cowardly wimp. In fact, any committed attempt made to disidentify yourself from your fears deserves to be called strong and courageous.

As you begin to disidentify with paralyzing fear, you'll start to have more control over your life. Gradually, you will learn to see yourself as more powerful than your fears. Moving from reacting *to* your fear to acting *on* it allows you to be much more independent and authentic.

Here's an exercise in disidentification: The next time you're aware of feeling afraid, discover and acknowledge what you fear, accept that it's something present with you at the moment, and then repeat several times to yourself: I have a fear of (heights, failure, e-mail, etc.), but *I* am not this fear!

We have come to believe that we are what we feel. But it's not true. Feelings are absolutely important, but they aren't the totality of who we are. We are much, much more than our feelings. You might try this further exercise: Think of some sentences that appeal to you as accurate definitions of who you are. For example:

I am a wise and wonderful woman.

I am a pure center of self-consciousness.

I am perfectly okay as is.

I am too amazing to fathom.

I am a child of God.

I'm okay even though I make mistakes.

Then choose the sentence that is most powerful to you (or make up your own) and add it to the preceding disidentification affirmation. For example, I might say, "I have a fear of rejection, but I am not this fear. I am a beautiful, unique soul created in God's image." Use whatever works for you. This is a simple but extremely powerful tool to keep you from being sucked into the vortex of your fear.

BURIED FEARS

We can't always be protected as we're growing up, so it's inevitable that we've had experiences ranging from rather scary to completely terrifying. When something happens to us as small children, we often have no way to verbalize our feelings thereby letting others know that we need help and healing. Children who can communicate their feelings, whether through bad behavior or a good, healthy scream, are the lucky ones. Less fortunate are those children who repress frightening incidents, shutting them away from conscious awareness.

Up to approximately age seven, children often feel responsible for the events that happen in their lives. If a parent dies, or if their parents argue, the young child feels it must be his or her fault. The child's developing ego structure is not yet able to perceive cause and effect as pertaining to others. Because children see themselves as the center of the universe, the pivotal point around which all events revolve, they tend to assume responsibility for whatever takes place. As a result, children who repress their fears usually end up feeling not only fearful but bad and unworthy as well.

The story of Victoria is a good case in point. As an adult, Victoria appeared to be well adjusted and successful. She had a good education, a fulfilling job, children, and a supportive husband. She came from an apparently loving though straight-laced and repressive family. When she entered therapy, she was suffering from continuous nightmares, a crushing fear of going to bed alone, chronically low self-esteem, and acute suicidal tendencies. She felt crazy, and the question "Why?" haunted her.

Victoria blamed herself for not snapping out of her depression. After losing an alarming amount of weight and thinking constantly of suicide, she sought therapy. With support from her husband and from me as her therapist, and with tremendous courage on her part, she allowed a series of long-buried memories to rise to conscious awareness.

Beginning in infancy, Victoria had been repeatedly sexually molested and physically threatened. Because her fear was so great and her sense of shame and guilt so powerful, she had repressed all conscious awareness of these atrocities. Not until she was thirty-six years old and faced with overwhelming personal crises did her defenses begin to crumble.

Painful as Victoria's memories were, it was extremely important that they emerge from hiding, from the dungeons where she'd kept them locked away. Now there was a known reason for her seemingly groundless fears. She was not crazy, as she had thought. The fears she'd experienced were entirely appropriate, considering what she had endured as a child. At last healing could begin.

Our fears are clues that there are hidden reservoirs of pain inside us in need of healing. As you can see from the extreme example of Victoria, unresolved fears can be debilitating, even life threatening. Having the courage to search for the source of our fears is a necessary first step toward being who we really are, free from limitations and able to express our fullest potential.

SHINING THE LIGHT OF PRAYER

If you are experiencing fears that seem rootless, out of all proportion to the apparent cause, or having no "logical" basis, give yourself a priceless gift: explore them. While a large percentage of such fears can be overcome only if they are brought out of the dungeon, I've discovered a wonderful thing since *The Courage to Be Yourself* was first published. In many cases, the light and energy of prayer can transform fear without each nitty-gritty detail being brought into the light of conscious awareness.

I had a client whom I'll call Sally. As Sally shared her story, it became apparent that the likelihood of her being an incest survivor was huge. All the telltale symptoms were there. Gently, I broached questions about her father and live-in relatives. No memories surfaced. Believing that prayer is a powerful agent of change, I suggested its use to Sally. She readily agreed.

To give Sally a focal point for her prayers, we did a guided meditation in which she felt her fear and created a symbol for it. From a safe and protected place, she began to imagine a warm, loving, and forgiving light flowing in, around, and through herself and the symbol of fear. For Sally, results were immediate. Bathed in light, the symbol seemed less loathsome and terrifying. Within weeks of faithfully using this visual prayer, Sally's free-floating fear and anxiety were almost gone. Nary a memory had surfaced, nor a dragon peeked from the cave's entrance.

Maybe I was wrong about incest as a probability. It doesn't matter. In Sally's case, the light of prayer found its way into the cave of her unconscious and transformed the resident fear. Sally's healing is not an isolated incident. Prayer, especially visual prayer, has been incredibly transformative in my own life and in the lives of many of the women I know.

That being said, it's still important to explore fear. As a general rule, as long as fear remains hidden, we are held captive in its clutches. We would be well advised to always bring light to our explorations. It can be done as simply as murmuring a "Please help me" before we begin or as elaborately as a full-fledged guided visualization. Remember, light dispels darkness.

EXPLORING FEAR

To see and know the worst is to take
from Fear her main advantage.

CHARLOTTE BRONTË

Fear feeds on darkness and secretiveness. Those of us who have learned to *beware* of fear instead of *being aware* of it need to remember that awareness allows us to choose what to do with our fear and provides an otherwise unavailable avenue for healing it.

One of the reasons it's so difficult for us to look at our fears is that we were never encouraged to do so. Watching our parents deny their fears and then act them out in oblique ways taught us to do the same. We learned to project our fears outside ourselves. Instead of saying, "I get scared and feel abandoned when you raise your voice at me," we yell back in order to silence the source of fear outside ourselves. Or we cower and acquiesce while concealing anger and hurt inside. Either reaction only intensifies negative feelings.

Often we women are in a double bind: we fear failure, but we also fear success. In relationships, we experience fear due to insecurity. We fear we're not good enough, smart enough, slim enough, sexy enough, or caring enough. If we aren't earning enough money, we fear we're not doing our part; if we make too much money, we're afraid our affluence might threaten other people. We fear we do too much for our children, thus spoiling them and making them dependent; we fear we aren't doing enough for our kids, and they feel neglected. When we're young, we fear we don't have enough experience and credibility. As we grow older, we fear the loss of our youthful appeal.

It's important to note that most hidden fears are stashed away because at one time it seemed safer to hide them than to be aware of them. As you begin to explore your fear, you may experience the original feelings again. Therefore, it's essential to protect yourself via prayer, or whatever methods work for you, before examining fear. You must be convinced that the risk you're taking in exposing the origin of your fears is something you can safely handle. Before you begin to dig deeply, find a person or group with whom you feel safe, and whom you can trust implicitly with your vulnerability. In my women's group, we often ask to be held in the light as we excavate fear or navigate crises. Being surrounded by loving energy helps no matter what the circumstance.

Since the origin of our fears most often lies in childhood, we can expect to experience childlike fear while rediscovering them. Seeking emotional support at such times is not dependency; it is wisdom. Wouldn't you think it self-defeating if a friend were run over by a truck but wouldn't allow doctors to set her broken bones or friends to aid her in her convalescence? Letting others nurture and support us helps us heal more quickly. When we're run over by an emotional truck, it's silly to think we shouldn't burden other people. The facade of stiff-upper-lip encourages repression, not healing. Repression imprisons. Healing frees.

With that caveat expressed, let's begin to take the fear dragons out of the dungeon. Because it often helps to have a format when we begin something new or scary, I've provided the following exercise as a guide.

1. Fears I have overcome:

    a._____

    b._____

    c._____

2. Fears I have almost conquered:

    a._____

    b._____

    c._____

3. Fears that limit my life now.

    a._____

    b._____

    c._____

4. Fears I pretend I don't have:

    a._____

    b._____

    c._____

5. Fears I have never had:

   a._____

   b._____

   c._____

6. Fears I wouldn't look at if promised a million dollars
   (prayer may be the only option for these):

   a._____

   b._____

   c._____

7. What is the worst thing that could happen if I recognized
   hidden fears?

   a._____

   b._____

   c._____

8. Fears I want to work on now:

   a._____

   b._____

   c._____

9. Freedoms I look forward to having when my fears
    are healed:

    a._____

    b._____

    c._____

Please, if feelings threaten to "run you over" as you explore
your fears, find a hand to hold or a group to provide ballast,
insight, support, and light.

FEAR CREATES REALITY

In ways that most of us don't fully understand, fear is like a
magnet that attracts to us the things we fear the most. For
instance, if we fear public speaking—and it is said this is the
most prevalent fear we have—and approach the podium
quaking in our boots and deathly afraid we'll forget our message,
it is likely we will have a lapse of memory. If our mind is tuned to
an internal channel that consistently repeats fearful litanies,
fear will be our experience. But we can change the channel.
One helpful technique to neutralize such magnetism is to avoid
negative statements that begin with "I am," such as:

I am fearful.

I am unlovable.

I am unemployable

I am old and worn out.

I am always sick.

I am ugly.

Such statements are self-fulfilling. If we wear negative name tags, we'll attract negative company.

Instead of resorting to "I am" statements when talking about our fears, we can make a simple change to:

I have a fear of (rejection, etc.).

I sometimes feel unlovable.

At times I feel old and ugly.

I have a fear of (failure/success/whatever).

When I stand up in front of a group, I feel (nervous, tongue-tied, dumb).

With such statements, you acknowledge that you have fears, but you don't identify yourself as being a manifestation of them. The difference is subtle but important. You have fears, and you can heal them. You are not your fears.

As you learn to heal your fears, you'll also learn to act without letting them limit you. These days, whenever I notice a fear crying out in my body, I say, "Thanks, Body, I hear you." Then I check it out to see if the fear is currently valid or an old response. If it is a familiar, much-worked-on pattern, I say a variation of, "Okay, old friend, I'm going to act as if you aren't here and do what I need to do now."

Too often, an unrealistic expectation about fear prevents us from acting. We believe we should never feel fearful and so try waiting until we feel perfectly at ease before tackling the difficulty or challenge that lies before us. This strategy never works. Many of our accomplishments happen in spite of fear.

In fact, in many instances, anxiety and fear can actually propel us into action.

Bill Russell, retired Boston Celtics player, was one of the all-time greats of pro basketball. Yet he would get so nervous before each game that he'd vomit. Nonetheless, he never let his fear keep him from being a world-class player. He used his talent to the utmost despite his fears.

For the first few years after I began giving talks and leading seminars, each time I stood up in front of a group, I felt terrified. Perspiration soaked me down to the waistband and nausea threatened to really embarrass me and deeply inconvenience whoever was introducing me. Over time, I learned to reassure myself I had something worthwhile to say, do a little yoga/breathing/affirmation exercise, and start talking. Now once I get into the swing of it, I have a great time. It's almost as if the energy generated by my fear propels me into doing a better job.

Some of my before-talk fright came from experience. At a high-school "Lit Night" where all of the literary clubs competed in speeches, monologues, and poetry readings, I was to do a funny monologue about girdles (remember those?). The girl who recited before me forgot her lines, and my reaction was cold-sweat terror that I'd forget also. Sure enough, my brain went numb. Though I knew my lines perfectly, I had tuned my mind to a panic channel and my fearful inner dialogue created what I feared. The memory of my embarrassed mother sliding farther and farther down in her seat as she mouthed the words to me was branded in my brain for years.

As the preceding story demonstrates, this statement from the Bible expresses a deep truth: "Lo, the thing I feared the most has come to pass." If we fear illness, we are likely to become ill. If we fear abandonment and rejection, we will most likely experience them in our lives. Speaking for myself, when I fear rejection, I approach people guardedly, inevitably making them feel that I'm cool or unfriendly and my very fear causes the rejection I'm trying so hard to protect myself from.

One effective way to overcome fear is to take one tiny little step at a time in spite of it. Taking small steps despite fear is called "desensitization." As we persevere and *do*, in spite of fear, fear begins to lose its grip on us.

Robin, a client of mine, was afraid to drive out of town. In the safety of my office, we began to desensitize her by having her close her eyes and imagine herself driving. If anxiety arose, we did relaxation techniques. When she could visualize herself on the street and driving away from home without anxiety, she took another small step. While sitting in the driveway in her car, she visualized herself driving around town. When she felt able to move on to another small step, she drove about a mile from home. With small, successful steps, she mastered her fear and now feels fine driving almost anywhere.

ERASING "IF ONLY"

Ralph Waldo Emerson said, "Fear always springs from ignorance." While I agree with Mr. Emerson, I think the opposite is also true: ignorance springs from fear. And, interestingly, the first letters of these two words, ignorance and fear, create one of the biggest little words in the English language: if.

We can look at the word "if" as a combination of ignorance and fear. When we are ignorant of our own worth, lovability, and creativity, when we fear that we are not doing/being enough, or when we fear almost anything excessively and/or obsessively, a life-leveling litany of "if onlys" runs through our minds: "If only I were smarter... ; if only I had a different parent, partner, or child... ; if only I were more like... ; if only I had... if only I hadn't... if only they... if only, if only, if only."

Being ignorant of the possibilities within us and fearful of taking the risks involved in seeing and acting on our possibilities almost guarantees that "only" will follow "if" in our emotional vocabulary.

If we have a lifelong legacy of fear, the task before us is to outgrow that limiting inheritance, erase "if onlys" from our lives, and claim our true birthright: the freedom to be ourselves. We can courageously free ourselves by facing our fears and altering our beliefs born of ignorance.

Freedom comes from knowing that though fear can't be avoided, it can be faced, lived through, learned from, and prayed for. While fear dragons will inevitably express themselves, it is up to us whether they do so honestly and overtly, which enhances self-esteem, or dishonestly and covertly, which undermines emotional strength. Each time we challenge a fear—walk into the middle of it with support from others, if need be—it diminishes and we experience more emotional independence. Gathering the courage to face fear helps us believe in ourselves and gives us confidence in our ability to cope with and triumph in any circumstance.

CHAPTER EIGHT

FACES OF FEAR

I know how cold and paralyzing fear can be. I know
how much strength, courage, and hard work are
needed to conquer it. Most of all, I know that there
are few victories in life more liberating than the
victory over the low, dark clouds of fear that block
our spirits from their rightful place in the sun.

SYLVIA BROWNE

I f we have not yet conquered our fears, much of our time is
spent reacting automatically rather than acting creatively
and appropriately. The tyranny of fear keeps us tied to outmoded
patterns of behavior. Not recognizing our internal dragons of
fear allows them to indulge their nasty habit of emerging from
their caves in destructive forms. I call these unconscious and
recurring themes the "faces of fear."

Fear wears many faces, and we each have fears that are
unique to us. I've chosen to discuss seven ways of disguising
fear that I've found to be almost universal among the women
with whom I've worked. Exploring these common faces of
fear—and how we act as a result of them—gives us a model for
transforming fear into positive and growth-producing energy.
Fear *can* act as an impetus rather than an impediment.

The seven faces of fear are:

- Appeasing
- Compulsive Action
- Exhaustion
- Resistance
- Addiction
- Illness
- Depression

APPEASING

Dictionary definitions of *appease* include "to pacify; give in to the demand, either silent or spoken, of another." My own definition is "to try to make 'it' okay for the other guy, to take responsibility for his or her life, to placate at the expense of yourself, your freedom, and your feelings of self-esteem." Sounds a lot like co-dependence and emotional dependence, doesn't it? Feels like it too!

For many women, appeasing is a familiar pattern. How often do we acquiesce to our children's demands when we really don't believe they're reasonable? Or appease the man in our lives by giving in to his moods and desires, even if it doesn't feel right for us?

We often do this with men because from the get-go society provides boy children with a sense of entitlement that girl children are less likely to receive. A friend and I were chuckling—chuckling is sometimes far superior to cringing or raging—over the idea of masculine entitlement and she said, "I know exactly what you mean! Ray has learned to say 'Excuse me' as he elbows his way past one of us to the kitchen cabinets, but we all know he means 'Get out of my way!'" Seemingly society has given many men the assurance that when they want the cereal, it's their right to have it *now*. The smile I write this with now has been hard earned and a long time coming, I can assure you. Smiling about entitlement was not—and still isn't—possible when I had only a tenuous grasp on being myself or felt emotionally vulnerable.

The need for connection is another reason women are so prone to appeasing behavior. The desire for connection is inherent in girls. Author of *In A Different Voice* and Harvard University researcher, Carol Gilligan studied preschool children and found that even at that early age, girls were much more appeasing than boys. Girls wouldn't disagree over the rules of a game but would try to make peace in order to preserve the relationships among their playmates. When arguments erupted, boys needed to honor the rules of the game and would sacrifice closeness with their peers in order to maintain their stance. Gilligan concluded that girls more than boys, for whatever reasons, value emotional connectedness.

As adults, women appease their own need for emotional connectedness by giving themselves away. It's as if we feared "death by disconnection."

We try to appease people because we fear rejection, disapproval, and separation. Confrontation scares us. We feel uncomfortable when we disagree. Our stomachs churn and our throats tighten with fear. We're afraid that "they" may disagree with us, disapprove of us, dislike us, reject us, or even leave us. We dread feeling emotionally separated and abandoned.

Early in our lives, we women learn to "make nice" in order to appease those with whom we want to stay connected. When we were children, our parents' disapproval felt life threatening. As we grew older, we transferred our emotional, and sometimes economic, dependence from parents to peers, boyfriends, mates, and government agencies.

Although women are making great strides toward economic independence, financial dependence remains a reality that often keeps us in unhappy and unhealthy situations. Even if we are independently wealthy, emotionally it can feel life threatening to be out of favor with our mates, children, coworkers, or friends. Through fear of emotional isolation, we too easily give up our autonomy.

Not only do women have a need for closeness, we have a natural penchant for peacemaking. Many of us consider it our job to be the emotional lighthouse for those around us. Whenever someone seems to be in danger of hitting the rocks emotionally, we feel it's our duty to jump in and rescue them. Sometimes this is a great gift to offer, but if we appease in order to purchase peace at any price, we are giving ourselves away.

Do you sacrifice your well-being in order to keep the peace in your family or at work? If so, do you find yourself inwardly seething and feeling resentful and ripped off? If you do, the price you are paying is lack of inner peace and low self-esteem. Quite a concession.

Women often say in response to their own feelings, needs, and wants, or to a hurtful remark made carelessly, "Oh, well, I'll let that pass. It's not worth the effort to deal with it." What we're really saying is, "*I'm* not worth the effort." We are the only caretakers of our feelings of worth and self-esteem. Consciously or unconsciously we teach people how to treat us. When we don't feel worthy, it's uncanny how those around us see us as unworthy and begin to use us as emotional dishrags to clean up all their messes. This kind of dependence is excruciating. I know, because I was a chronic appeaser.

In my deep inner self, in the scared little girl I carried with me, I feared I would die if I were rejected. So I avoided confrontation. I remember a time when a friend hurt my feelings through a joking remark made in the company of others. I was crushed because she had jabbed one of my most vulnerable areas, but I smiled to cover my hurt and let the remark go. I even felt a little guilty for being hurt and angry as if, somehow, I caused the remark. Thankfully that is not likely to happen now. Through therapy and honest talks with myself and with friends, I've learned to love and comfort my inner child whenever she feels rejected. Now I let her know she won't die, because she can always count on *me* to be there for her emotionally. With my inner child protected, I am able to clear up misunderstandings or hurts between myself and others.

I often see appeasing behavior in other women, especially in relation to their mates. I recently watched a friend try repeatedly to mollify her husband. She had wanted to go to a concert, and he agreed to go with her. During the performance, she kept checking with him to see if he was enjoying it. If she sensed that he was disgruntled, she would rub his back and talk cajolingly to him as if to say, "Please, please enjoy yourself, so that I can enjoy myself." Later she became aware of the fear that had prompted her behavior. Whenever her husband disapproves, he withdraws into icy moodiness or uses verbal ridicule. She felt if he were bored, she would have hell to pay for suggesting they go. Her life with him is a vicious circle: the fear of his reaction causes her to appease him, which in turn makes her mad at herself and him.

Appeasing behavior is the negative face of a very powerful talent that women can offer to the world, that of nurturing people and making intimate connections with them. I've learned not to appease, but I do compromise. Appeasing behavior comes from a fearful, powerless place inside of us, a place where there is very little choice. On the other hand, conscious compromise comes from our adult, empowered self, the part of us that knows we have the ability to choose. If we are in relationships with others, there will always be times when compromising is appropriate, but we need to do so from a center of inner honesty and integrity—a place of strength and flexibility. That's a far cry from giving yourself away.

Appeasing isn't an easy habit to break. The first step is to become aware of doing it. When you think about this, try to be very specific. Exactly how do you appease? And whom do you appease? Is it your husband, children, mother/father-in-law, or coworkers? When you become aware of appeasing behavior, stop and pay attention to how you feel. Like everyone else who appeases, you'll probably discover that, beneath the motivational fear, you feel resentful, angry, and embarrassed.

Once you've become aware of your appeasing behavior, you can choose to act in a different way. The old yearning to appease will still be present, but as you continue to act in a respectful and authentic way toward yourself and others, the need to appease will gradually dissipate.

The trick to changing appeasing behavior is to increase your tolerance for emotional separation. When you can learn to say to yourself, "Oh well, I see we'll be separate for a little while now. How can I take care of myself in that time?", then you'll have begun to break the chain that binds you to appeasing behavior.

As I was changing my need to appease, it was important for me to put some distance between myself and the persons from whom I felt emotionally separated. When I stayed in close proximity to them, the urge to overcome my pain through appeasing behavior was almost overwhelming. So I took care of myself by getting out of the house.

What can you do when you feel rejected or disconnected and need to strengthen your sense of self-esteem? Call a friend. Go to a movie. Commune with nature. Write in your journal. Talk to and take care of your inner child. Face your fears squarely, and then choose to stop the automatic, destructive behaviors they usually evoke. You will not die. You will survive.

Acknowledge your feelings to the person or persons involved. If that isn't possible, or if it wouldn't be constructive, tell your feelings to a friend or to a therapist—even to your dog or cat, if necessary—or express them in a private journal. Accept the fact that you've been an appeaser and that you can choose to behave differently now.

Periods of change are full of paradoxes. They're difficult but exciting, frightening but freeing. Letting go of old patterns that no longer work for us is exhilarating. As we learn to replace appeasing behavior with assertive, self-valuing patterns, we begin to feel mature and equal in our relationships. Study the fears that keep you appeasing: look at them, examine them, bring them out into the open. As you learn about them and consciously adopt positive counter-behaviors, your fears will dissipate and you'll break out of the cycle of appeasement.

COMPULSIVE ACTION

The trend among most people I know under the age of sixty is toward compulsive action. It's as if our lives are on a treadmill with the continually increasing speed outside our control.

The pace of our lives at work, home, and play anesthetizes us to the real reasons for each: Why do we work? Why do we try so hard to create a good home? Why do we play? Before we can answer these questions, we need to ask some others: Why do I run so fast? What am I running toward? What am I running from? Is this fast pace the way I really want to live? Who sets my breakneck pace?

Ruth, who could be the fast-pace poster girl, confessed, "I only feel in control when I am really busy. On those rare occasions when I stop doing something, I feel panicky, like I'm caught in the crosshairs of some cosmic rifle and have to escape."

I think Ruth's statement describes feelings many compulsive doers would identify with if they took the time to explore the way they feel. If you find yourself in Ruth's shoes (running shoes, of course), I urge you to see if fear is lengthening your stride and upping your daily mileage requirements.

Many women who have wrestled compulsive action to the ground, and won, have told me they discovered they were going at such a clip in order to avoid feeling and even being. Sad as this sounds, their basic bare-bones fear was this: "What if I stop to smell the roses and find I can't smell and there are no roses?" Or worse, "What if I stop, look, and listen to myself and see and hear *nothing?* What if I am a void?" No one is a void, but when we a-void ourselves by running away, we can definitely feel empty.

If we are attempting to avoid that kind of angst and low self-esteem, there is much emotional and spiritual work to be done in order to recover and rebuild a sense of self.

If you are obsessively active, please at least pause to ask yourself why and to listen for the answer from the still, quiet voice alive and well within you. I don't have an answer for the hurry sickness afflicting our society and our souls. But I do trust that the how-to-stop-it is within you, and you can change your pace if you want to.

EXHAUSTION

If you find that you are always tired, the first thing to do is make sure you are medically okay. And, of course, juggling more and more commitments a day is bound to make us weary. But one of the quickest ways to become exhausted is by suppressing our feelings— burying them in the dungeon of our subconscious. This process has been called "gunnysacking." Anything we don't want to see or experience, we stuff into an emotional gunnysack.

As we hide more and more feelings, the sack gets bigger and heavier. Carrying around an oppressive bag full of unresolved and unspoken feelings leaves us so fearful and drained that our emotional strength ebbs away and we have no energy left to stand up for ourselves.

If you're a sack toter, it's no small wonder you feel exhausted. It's very tiring to lug around a bag of fears, hurts, and disappointments, holding tight to the drawstring so they won't sneak out and overwhelm you or attack someone else. It's like sitting on a trapdoor through which many rebellious gremlins are trying to rise.

If chronic fatigue is an issue in your life, it may be that you're harboring feelings that need to be looked at and moved through. It's much harder work for our minds and bodies to avoid the feelings that need attention—to stuff them down, ignore them, or put off dealing with them—than it is to face them. It takes an enormous amount of energy to hide from ourselves and others the dark feelings and thoughts we all have.

We say to ourselves, "Maybe if I ignore it, it'll go away." But of course it doesn't. Our unacknowledged feelings merely grow bigger, more ruthless, and uncontrollable. In the long run, facing feelings is less work than avoiding them, and it is infinitely more rewarding.

Often exhaustion is a signal from our wise body and mind alerting us to hidden feelings. If you feel too threatened by your buried feelings to uncover them alone, seek professional guidance. Your fatigue is telling you it's time to lighten the inner load.

RESISTANCE

It's human nature to resist what we fear. Resistance is quite clever. Whenever we're challenged to change, this face of fear hides behind righteous indignation at how unfair and unfeeling people and circumstances are.

Some people resist everything—from the weather, fate, and aging to ball scores, their spouses, and politics. We think of such people as negative and grumpy; in reality, they're afraid. They fear everything that involves risk, change, or loss of control. Rather than look within themselves and change their own reactions, they blame the world outside.

Resistance loves to put on disguises:

"I forgot...."

"They didn't call me."

"I overslept."

"I'm too tired."

"It doesn't matter anyway."

"Why change? It's okay the way it is."

"It's too hard."

"I could never do that!"

"You shouldn't feel that way."

"That's dumb!"

"Isn't it awful?"

"I'm too fat (too old, too anything) for that!"

"I can't."

"Why is it always me who has to change?"

The best way to overcome resistance is to gently push on it. When you notice yourself becoming negative, laugh about it if you can. Magnify your gripes until they become ridiculous. The more lightly you deal with your resistance, the easier it'll be to move through it. Look at your resistance and, from the wiser, lighter part of your mind, choose to act anyway.

When I began to write this book, I came face to face with gigantic obstacles of resistance. After all, what did I have to say that would be worthwhile to anybody? They might laugh at my efforts. And just think of the sheer work involved!

My insecure inner self stepped forward and sneered when I lost my tape recorder and the notes of my first meeting with my publicist. (I'd put them on top of the car and they scattered all over the road as I drove away.) I realized then that I was anxious about writing the book—*terrified* is a better word—and I spoke about it aloud. I honored the fear and didn't act on it. I stopped resisting the long process of writing and promised myself I would take it one small step at a time. Working through my initial resistance was essential. If I hadn't dealt with it, the book would never have been completed.

Sharon, a client of mine, told me, "I've been really bothered by something you said last week." I had told her to gently look at any resistance she had toward therapy. She was convinced she wasn't resisting. She said she loved our time together; and yet, she was ten minutes late to her first session, and twenty minutes late to the second because her "husband wouldn't hurry." She missed the third session altogether, and was late again to the fourth.

As we talked about her behavior, she agreed that, yes, it was scary to come to therapy and she feared what she might find out about herself. Consciously she was eager to learn and grow; subconsciously she was frightened. As soon as she became aware of her resistance, she no longer needed to be late. She acknowledged her fear to herself and to me, and we both accepted it whenever it arose. She is learning to let it go, piece by piece.

Resistance is a twisted expression of a natural tendency. After all, there are many situations in which we really must protect ourselves. To strip away our healthy sense of caution suddenly and entirely would be like pulling off a protective scab. Therefore, as you begin to work on your inner resistance, do so gently, patiently, and with love.

ADDICTION

Thanks to courageous people like Betty Ford, we have become increasingly aware of our society's tendency toward addictions of all kinds: overeating, alcohol, drugs (prescription, over the counter, and illegal), and overworking, to name a few. The list could go on almost indefinitely.

If we are hiding our fears in addiction of some kind, our first reaction will probably be, I'm not addicted to _____! One of the major symptoms of addiction is denial. Has this so-called nonexistent problem ever evoked concerned remarks from your family and friends? If so, you need to pay close attention to what it is you're trying to deny.

Hiding our fears behind compulsive behavior of any kind severely limits our ability to be ourselves. If addiction is a problem for you, there is help around every corner: you have only to find the courage to reach out and ask. Scores of groups such as Alcoholics Anonymous, Al-Anon, Narcanon, and Overeaters Anonymous meet daily in almost every city and town. If you feel more comfortable working on your own, bookstores are teeming with excellent recovery books. Do yourself a life-saving favor and find the help you need.

Besides being addicted to chemicals, many of us compulsive doers have become addicted to chaos and calamity. Why? Because if we are swept up in a torrent of activities or traumas, it takes all of our energy just to stay afloat and we don't have to realize that our lives are not our own nor do we need to take responsibility for them. We have neither the time nor the energy to say, "Is this all there is to life?"

We aren't to blame for our fears, but it is up to us to decide how we'll handle them. We are responsible for choosing ways that lead us toward making the most of this gift of life. Our main job is to realize who and what we are and to express our beauty in the world. We can't do that if we are either deadened or overstimulated by addictions.

ILLNESS

Repressed feelings tend to lodge in the body in the form of hidden tensions, unhealthy habits, and stress-induced chemical changes. Often illness is an expression of feelings repressed.

Carl and Stephanie Simonton of the Simonton Cancer Center in Pacific Palisades, California, found that when terminally ill patients expressed their gunnysacked feelings of guilt, rage, fear, and other difficult feelings, their cancer frequently went into remission, or at least their symptoms became less acute. Dr. Bernie Siegel, a surgeon who uses love as often as a scalpel, encourages his patients to verbalize explicitly all of their feelings. An amazing number of Dr. Siegel's "terminal" patients get well.

Our bodies try to communicate with us, but all too often we don't pay attention to the signals they send. When we ignore it, our body grabs our attention in creative ways. Marge's story is a perfect example. She was going through an extremely stressful family situation and felt depleted by the emotional strain. Through exhaustion and increased muscle tension, her body told her to take time to rest and replenish her energies. She ignored its message and buried herself in work and commitments, pushing herself beyond the brink.

She began to lose weight dramatically. All her clothes hung on her and her coworkers were forever presenting their "Twiggy" with bagels and donuts, but she didn't have time to eat. One day she fainted in the post office and woke up to find herself surrounded by the concerned faces of paramedics and post-office patrons. Being a very private person, she was mortified. As Marge was being whisked away to the hospital, she made a commitment to begin listening to her body. It turned out to be a life-saving commitment because not long after her fainting spell, she found a lump in her breast and immediately had it checked. Though the tumor was malignant, she had discovered it early enough to save both her breast and her life.

Illness is a great way to resist. It seems so socially acceptable and might even get us some sympathy. Whenever Wyn and her husband fight, she gets flu symptoms. She fears him and her own feelings. By getting sick she avoids further confrontation. Her unexplored feelings come out in the form of physical symptoms. Unfortunately her inability to face her fears creates a lose-lose situation for herself and her husband. It spares her the discomfort of confrontation but leaves them both frustrated, angry, and confused. She's left with physical symptoms and unresolved issues in her marriage, and she remains the uncomfortable target of his anger and frustration.

Our bodies forewarn us. Several years ago, I was sick for ten days straight—and I'm rarely sick. I had ignored many clear warning signs, and finally my overworked body said, "Okay, Sue, you asked for it," and simply quit. I couldn't go on. For four or five days, all I could do was rest. Even reading was too strenuous. As my energy seeped back, I began to ask why I needed this illness. It became obvious to me that I'd been feeling responsible for the lives of everyone around me. I'd convinced myself that my clients couldn't make it without me, and that my family needed my constant support, listening ear, and ready sense of humor. I was indispensable.

Besides being an expression of a genuine desire to help my friends and family, my compulsion was an ego trip. I pushed and pushed: Xena to the rescue. But Xena finally fell off her horse and into her bed and stayed there. Surprise! Everyone to whom I'd felt indispensable got along just fine. Clients survived, my professional life came back to normal quickly, the family marched right along, friends took care of their own lives, organizations found other volunteers, and my body got its much-needed rest. Pattern broken—or at least severely cracked.

The fear that led me to get sick was that if I didn't give my all, always, I wouldn't be good enough; and if I weren't good enough, surely I would be unloved and abandoned. Clients would leave, children would feel neglected, husband would be disappointed. I wouldn't be *perfect*. It took illness to show me that I'd reverted to two old patterns familiar to many women: (1) taking care of everyone else first; and (2) being perfect in order to be okay.

An essential part of a happy, healthy life is being of service to others, but *indispensable is destructive.* Pace yourself in your work and commitments. Nobody is indispensable. And when you get sick, honor your body by giving it the rest and medical attention that it's asking for.

Of course, not all illness is emotionally induced. A therapist friend of mine who was accustomed to self-evaluation developed a severe headache during an aerobics class. She asked herself all the usual questions: "Why do I need this? What am I not looking at? What do I need to learn from this headache?" No answers came. Was she hiding something from herself? Almost as an afterthought she loosened her headband. That worked.

Be gentle with yourself. If you discover that you're using illness as an escape, or pushing yourself until you get sick, learn to change that behavior. Honor your body before it gets ill. And, if it does give out because it needs a rest, relax and enjoy it.

DEPRESSION

Depression is the classic disease of women. Change two letters and instead of *de*pression you have *ex*pression. If we don't express what we're feeling—what's bugging us—in a constructive, healing manner, very often the result is depression: the way women weep without tears.

Depression is like a fog that settles over us, limiting our ability to see what we're really feeling. Often when we're depressed there's something we need to do about a particular situation, and we're afraid to do it.

Some kinds of depression are normal. When we experience a loss, a setback, or a shattered dream, it would be unnatural not to feel a bit depressed. But most depression, and certainly chronic depression (unless due to a chemical imbalance), is a sign that we have turned our unwanted feelings against ourselves and are avoiding something. Often, that "something" is anger.

In the psychology trade, there's an old cliche: depression is inverted anger. That's more or less true, but depression can also be inverted anything else. I don't know about you, but when I was growing up it was not okay for me to express anger. In our family, we denied that anger existed. I felt it, in myself and coming from my parents and sister, but we did not acknowledge it. We kept it locked out of sight, where it got bigger and bigger.

I remember giving in to anger once as a teenager and swore within hearing distance of my mother. Looking back, I feel it was reasonable anger and worthy of a good shout and a swear word or two. But the punishment for expressing my anger in that way was being forbidden to attend a dance that I had looked forward to. Also, Mother didn't speak to me for the rest of the day. So I learned to invert my anger to avoid rejection and punishment.

In order to save ourselves from the purgatory of disconnection we may have learned that:

Nice girls **don't** talk that way.

Nice girls **don't** act aggressive.

Nice girls **don't** rebel.

Nice girls **don't** get angry.

Unfortunately:

Nice girls **do** learn to play the victimized, poor-me role.

Nice girls **do** learn to express their anger covertly, in manipulative ways.

Nice girls **do** *get depressed.*

If you are depressed, check and see if, down deeper, you're really feeling angry. Anger is natural. It's how you tell yourself, "Whoa, something isn't right here." Although our culture mouths the axiom that all feelings are okay, we still get the message that anger and depression are "bad." Subconsciously the belief still thrives that nice, normal people are always upbeat and happy. Women especially seem to be shackled by this unspoken conviction.

We are only really depressed when we're not aware of our feelings. If we are aware of them and working through them, no matter what they are, we are in the process of healing.

There's a crucial point here. Don't label yourself or allow others to label you as depressed if you are in fact experiencing authentic feelings at the moment. I'm not talking about wallowing in self-pity—that's self-defeating. I am talking about taking out your fears and angers and looking at them. That's not depression.

If you feel depressed, get specific: What are you feeling? Name it. Bring the dragon out into the light.

Sondra felt depressed and didn't know why. With gentle exploration, we uncovered her real feeling: sadness. She was sad over the realities of a marriage in which her husband wasn't able to understand many of her feelings and needs. She felt alone, frustrated, and unhealthy. She had covered her sadness and loneliness with vague depression because she feared that voicing her real feelings would lead to a divorce.

As a result of our working together, she discovered what she wasn't getting out of the marriage and set about finding ways to fill those needs for herself. She chose to stay in the marriage and concentrate on its many positive aspects. She gave up her frustrated dependence on her husband and her expectation that he would fill most of her needs. Taking responsibility for her life, she became a computer whiz, opened her own business, began to cultivate new relationships, and reconnected with friends she'd lost track of. Sondra's depression was a valuable clue that she was covering up important feelings and thereby limiting her life.

As we begin to explore our depression for underlying feelings such as anger, it's very important to remember that it's hard for people to be on the receiving end of the full force of someone else's wrath. That's one reason why it's crucial we learn to stop inverting our anger. It's self-destructive to hold it in until it comes out as depression or as an uncontrolled volcanic explosion. Slugging your mate or kicking the dog is not constructive, but it is constructive to punch a punching bag, knead some bread, or play an aggressive game of tennis.

We need to accept our anger, fear, or whatever undisclosed feelings we have, no matter how socially unacceptable they seem. We are human; therefore we will have the entire gamut of human feelings whether we think they are permissible or not. In a climate of acceptance we can learn to express our feelings in healthy and productive ways. As we expand our love, acceptance, and support for ourselves, we become stronger and less affected by the reactions and actions of others. This frees us from wearing the faces of fear that mask our real selves.

You can begin immediately to transform your fears by changing your thoughts. No matter how many times fear attacks you, keep affirming that those fears are not you and that someday you will completely overcome them. Gradually, day by day, your positive affirmations will grow in strength until they begin to push back those old barriers of fear. Remember: your fears are not you, and you are not them. You can diminish them. You can act in spite of them. You can be free.

Review your past in an atmosphere of healing gentleness and self-respect. You've already done a lot of courageous work: you've survived despite obstacles. Give yourself credit for your inborn heroism, and keep working to realize your birthright of emotional freedom and strength.

CHAPTER NINE

UNDERLYING ASSUMPTIONS AND HIDDEN BELIEFS

The first problem for all of us, men and women, is not to learn, but to unlearn.

GLORIA STEINEM

O ur deep, often unconscious beliefs and assumptions determine whether we have the courage to be ourselves or continuously cast about outside of ourselves hoping others will define who we are. In order to enhance our self-esteem and increase our emotional strength we need to explore our hidden beliefs and assumptions—how we acquired these hidden dragons, why we're afraid to look at them, and what we can do about them once we do find the courage to observe them.

THINGS WE'VE SWALLOWED WHOLE

As we grow up, we are exposed to the many attitudes, ideas, feelings, and prejudices held by our parents, families, and the society at large. We absorb and mimic what we see and feel around us. We are constantly inundated by stimuli, subliminal messages, and suggestions, many of which are detrimental to our inner growth and freedom:

> "You aren't the only pebble on the beach!"
>
> "If you can't say something nice, don't say anything at all."
>
> "You'll never be hung for your beauty."

These statements come from the book called *Momalies: As Mother Used to Say.* Many of us grew up hearing similar things, which were limiting because as children we believed them. We swallowed them whole. In my opinion, that book would be better entitled *Momma Lies.*

Why wouldn't we believe such statements? After all, young children have little discernment and depend on their parents, teachers, and other adults to teach them the truths about life. As we grow older, we receive further instruction:

> "It's a man's world."
>
> "Speaking your mind is unattractive."
>
> "It's impossible to break through the glass ceiling."
>
> "A woman's place is in the home."
>
> "Physical beauty is essential for happiness."
>
> (And more subtly) "Men are more valuable than women."

Although we have made great strides toward equality in the past several decades, we still need to dig out beliefs that keep us tripping over the roots of the family tree. As we uproot underlying assumptions, our actions can truly begin to match the beliefs we *think* we hold. For instance, studies about the differences between teachers' attention to boys and girls in elementary schools show that boys receive more attention, even when the teacher herself or himself believes she or he shows no favoritism. In fact, the teachers argue that they are consciously committed to giving each child the same amount and quality of attention and instruction regardless of gender. It was not until they viewed videos of themselves teaching that they realized they frequently unconsciously favored boys. If intelligent and loving people, who have dedicated themselves to the extremely important yet often thankless job of teaching, reinforce (however unconsciously) society's idea of male superiority, imagine where else we must get the same idea. No wonder our self-esteem is low and we regularly feel less-than.

Erroneous messages we swallow whole as children become our own underlying assumptions and implicit beliefs. We guide our lives accordingly by becoming emotionally dependent on other people because "they must know better than we do." Since most of these notions are hidden, we're unaware of the extent to which they rule our actions and reactions—unless we consciously search them out in order to transform them. *Underlying* is the operative word, as these assumptions are *under* our conscious awareness, and *lie* to us about reality. Freeing ourselves from limiting and devaluing beliefs is the key to living up to our potential and expressing our authenticity.

Our assumptions govern us much as an automatic pilot guides an airplane. For example, if we have the hidden beliefs that life is hard or sex is dirty, we will have feelings that correspond to those beliefs. Thus beliefs hidden from conscious awareness may emerge as unconsciously motivated actions. In fact our actions will reflect our hidden feelings.

On the occasion of Ann's engagement, her father gave her the only heart-to-heart talk they'd ever had. He thought she should be told that her mother was frigid and that the possibility existed that Ann might be as well.

Up until then Ann had enjoyed sex, though she had felt a little guilty about her pleasure. Since Ann had been told all her life that she was just like her mother, she feared she might also be frigid. She immediately tried to hide the thought from herself, but sex soon began to be a problem for her and her new husband. Only when her underlying assumptions and fears were brought to the surface, acknowledged, and accepted did she discover that she was in fact a healthy, sensual, and sexual woman. Dad had dished out the possibility of frigidity, and she had swallowed it whole.

Our unconscious assumptions generate attitudes and actions that influence our lives in ways we may be completely unaware of. They often shape our choices of husband, career, home, friends, and lifestyle.

Mary became aware that for years she had consistently chosen men who were less intelligent than she, usually men whom she could dominate. Consequently she regularly felt frustrated and intellectually isolated in her relationships.

Mary's father, who was mentally unbalanced, dominated her mother totally. Her mother's fear of upsetting him kept her in the role of victim. Even as a young girl, Mary was aware of her mother's rage and shame because of the inequality in the relationship. Mary had felt her mother's pain, concluded that all relationships were one-sided, and vowed she would never be the inferior partner. Although she had repressed this awareness, she acted it out in her adult relationships by choosing men to whom she felt superior. Until she discovered the underlying beliefs that were guiding her actions, Mary hadn't considered the possibility that she might live side by side with anyone as an equal partner.

How many times have you heard women say, "I just can't do (_____) or (_____)!" Here's an example of a widely held assumption: women aren't as good at math as men are. Studies of young children have shown that girls are naturally just as adept in math as boys are. However, as girls grow up and are subjected to subtle (and not-so-subtle) messages from teachers, parents, peers, and prejudiced literature, they believe the lie and begin to live "down" to others' expectations.

In grade school and early high school, I made all As in math and received the highest grade in my sophomore class on a standardized geometry test. Sometime after my sophomore year, though, I began to buy into the popular belief that girls can't do math. To this day, I feel as if the number section of my brain has been coated with Teflon.

As we uncover hidden beliefs that limit us and replace them with valid assumptions and realizations (which I have yet to do in regard to my hidden belief about my math ability), we take a giant step toward changing our behavior, our feelings, and our lives. By healing false assumptions and attitudes, we create whole new patterns of behavior for ourselves; we open doors toward being who we really are. Breaking out of limiting beliefs is not a selfish act, for each time we free ourselves from restrictions we create a pattern of growth that encourages others to travel into and heal their own wounded inner regions.

THE POWER OF BELIEFS

Each of us functions within a set of beliefs. In our lives, belief systems create order and structure. They make important decisions easier, and they provide the basis for our integrity, ethics, and philosophy. Our personalities are structured by the beliefs we learned from parents, teachers, friends, and the culture around us.

For a great many of us, our parents' spoken and unspoken beliefs have become our own. As adults we no longer need to be told right from wrong because our parents' voices are ingrained in us, telling us how to behave and what's expected of us.

Our beliefs also arise from the ways we interpret what we see and hear as we grow up. And it's interesting to note that our beliefs frequently are based far more on interpretation than on fact. Virginia always broke corncobs in two before boiling them. She never questioned the logic of that behavior until her son asked her about it one day. She did it because her mother did it. When he probed further, her son discovered that his grandmother had a very logical explanation: her pots were too small to accommodate the large ears of corn grown in their fields. Virginia's belief was a habit based not on an acknowledged truth but on her own, unexamined interpretation of her mother's actions as right and proper, whatever their origin.

Our belief systems can also be created from fear. If we fear rejection or disapproval, we may believe that it isn't safe to disagree with others. When our views run contrary to popular opinion, we may find it hard to speak our minds. Why? Because we fear the consequences.

The culture around us also propagates inaccurate beliefs, such as that men are more powerful than women or that men should make more money because they have families to support—a popular belief that statistics refute. (At least 30 percent of all households in America today are wholly supported by a woman, according to the Census Bureau. And I bet those statistics are low.)

We give lip service to the idea that a woman's work in the home is as important as a man's work—until it comes to assigning a dollar value to the tasks performed. Women too easily acquiesce to the prevalent belief that the money the husband brings home is his to mete out as he sees fit. The belief that we have no money of our own can keep us feeling dependent on the men in our lives, confused about our rights, and limited in our choices. A woman who believes she is powerless to have or make money will feel unable to stop destructive behavior in the home, including physical and emotional abuse.

Positive beliefs guide us; false beliefs handicap us. There are new beliefs circulating—such as, if you want it done well and right, ask a woman—but many of us still bear unconscious assumptions about ourselves and other women.

"Women are overemotional."

"Women are catty and gossipy."

"Women can't be trusted."

"Women can't keep a confidence."

"Women aren't as capable as men."

When my first husband left me for my "best" friend, I began to believe that women couldn't be trusted. Yet, with that one painful exception (and a few excruciating high-school traumas), that hadn't been my experience with women. I felt I couldn't trust them, yet my life was virtually filled with trustworthy women. My new belief created painful paradoxes in my life, and since the rational mind has difficulty with paradoxes, I buried the conflict in my subconscious— thereby creating some pretty irrational feelings toward my loyal friends. Fortunately the origins of my distrust began to dawn on me, and I was able to talk to my friends and free myself from the inner turmoil.

An extremely important part of our work toward emotional growth and change will come from examining our belief systems regarding all areas of life. Especially important are our beliefs about other women, because negative beliefs about our women friends will separate us from the very people who can share and empathize with us in our triumph over emotional dependence. All of us are in the process of evolving from second-class citizenship. When we isolate ourselves from other women, we are subtly isolating ourselves from ourselves.

To gain the courage to be yourself, you need to address the beliefs that are keeping you stuck where you are. What beliefs, assumptions, and attitudes are you holding onto even though they no longer enhance your life? It is possible to free yourself from worn-out beliefs and acquire ones that bring happiness, strength, and self-esteem.

What we believe we may become.

DEFAULT TO *AT* FAULT

If I could identify one core problem about the world,
it's that we've been taught to distrust ourselves.

SHAKTI GAWAIN

Because it's true that we become what we believe we are, it is crucial that we cancel out erroneous beliefs held about ourselves.

Psychologists have discovered that if children do not learn self-esteem and self-confidence early in life, they will always have unhealthy responses to difficult internal and external stimuli. If false beliefs are imprinted upon our subconscious minds early enough, they become our default position, much the same as a word processor automatically returns to the margin settings it has been programmed with unless instructed to do otherwise.

For instance, somehow in my early years I came to believe that everything was my fault and to fear that I always did things wrong. Feeling I must be at fault and wrong is my inner default position. During crisis or criticism, I can easily fall back into finding fault with myself. I *default* to *at* fault.

Although different than mine, Eve's default position is equally powerful. As the eldest child of irresponsible alcoholic parents, Eve's default is set on, "I have to control everything. No one else will do it if I don't." Until she learned the origin of her frantic feelings and began to alter her beliefs, Eve's need to control was stifling to her children and husband and also caused quite a ruckus on a committee or two she chaired.

In times of deep crisis or overwhelming stress, both Eve and I automatically revert to the lowest common denominator of our self-concepts. Because we've worked on transforming our harmful beliefs, our childish reactions of "I'm bad... I'm at fault" and "I have to fix this!" may only last a nanosecond before we can respond in an appropriate, adult manner. But the little girls within us still harbor an acquired default position that they need to move away from.

Although this idea may sound discouraging, the concept has actually been very freeing for me. Knowing that I naturally have a primary, automatic response that signals I'm bad, wrong, and at fault has freed me from the burden of guilt and shame I've carried for being "weak" and "a slow learner." Without the leg-irons of shame and guilt, I'm better able to work on strengthening my secondary self-loving and affirming responses.

While I fall back into finding fault with myself, your conditioned, primary responses might well be positive. Whether self-enhancing or self-defeating, your default position is likely to be different from either mine or Eve's. One of the best ways to discover your automatic, first response is to explore the seed sentences germinating within you.

SEED SENTENCES: WEEDS OR FLOWERS?

I believe in the old adage "Cleanliness is next to Godliness," but not as a reference to dirt under our nails or behind our ears. Clean thoughts are what we need to have in order to grow closer to our own souls.

Do your thoughts leave you feeling fresh and sweet, or do they slime your self-concept with a brackish film of criticism, doubt, and shame? Your thoughts are yours alone. No one can clean them up but you. Exploring the seed sentences planted within you is a great way to uproot weeds, clean up your mind, and plant some flower seeds.

Seed sentences are clusters of ideas, words, or scripts that we all create in order to keep us congruent with our underlying assumptions and hidden beliefs. If our seed sentences are self-affirming and supportive, we are naturally self-confident, creative, and excited about life. These I call "flower sentences." When sentences are derogatory, we are more likely to be emotionally vulnerable, have low self-esteem, and find it difficult to be ourselves. Definitely "weeds."

Most seed sentences remain unspoken, perhaps even subconscious. They are bits and pieces of ideas we've picked up along the way until they form the heart of our beliefs about ourselves. Seed sentences come from many sources—parents, mates, TV, movies, magazines, advertising—and contribute to our ideas of how we're supposed to live and what we can expect to receive from life and from others. Our lives, in effect, sprout from seed sentences we carry.

If all of our seed sentences blossomed into flowers, our lives would be gardens filled with beauty and grace. Unfortunately most of us have picked up weed seeds that grow into thistles and thorns, choking our spontaneity and the realization of our authentic selves.

Some examples of flower seed sentences:

"I am a worthwhile person."

"I deserve to be loved."

"I am lovable."

"I can do anything I set my mind to."

"I am proud to be a woman."

If seed sentences such as these are blooming in your subconscious, you probably have a wonderful life, filled with loving relationships. When you look in the mirror in the morning, you are happy with what you see.

Weed sentences, on the other hand, sound something like this:

"I can never do anything right."

"I don't deserve to be loved."

"I'm no good at (_____) or (_____)."

"Everyone handles things better than I do."

"I'm so ashamed of (_____)."

Constant use of weed sentences undoubtedly means you feel pretty down on yourself. When people try to love you, you question their motives. "How can they love *me?* They must not be very bright." Weed sentences go hand in hand with low self-esteem.

Brenda, a high-school senior, felt she was a loser. Her seed sentences were "I'm too fat," "Thunder Thighs is my name," "I'm too stupid [though she had an A-minus average]," and

"I'm not attractive to boys. I'll never find an awesome guy who will like me!"

With these weed sentences buzzing in her head, she had developed a caustic exterior that scared people away. Whenever she had a crush on a boy and he ventured to look past her tough facade, she began to consider him a geek. Anyone interested in her was surely a loser. This double bind kept her from having what she wanted.

In therapy, we began to pull some of her weed sentences and replace them with beautiful and more truthful flower sentences. Eventually she went off to college, leaving not one but two very nice young men sorry to see her go and a mother who was thrilled by her only daughter's newfound happiness and confidence.

Another person who demonstrated the power of seed sentences is Connie. On the afternoon when she received her master's degree, Connie remembered her first-grade teacher saying to her mother, "It's nice that Connie is pretty, because she's not very bright." She took that to heart, and no matter how good her grades were in school, she felt dumb. Her teacher's comment had become an internalized seed sentence: "I'm pretty, but I'm dumb." Quite a weed.

How do we pick up our packet of thought-seeds? People make the most unbelievably careless statements within the sensitive hearing of children: "She has a face only a mother could love." Or "You're about as graceful as a bull in a china shop." Children take such pronouncements as authoritative, because they come from people who are ten feet tall.

"But I was only teasing..." Ever hear that one? It didn't make you feel any better, did it? Teasing is veiled hostility and is almost never funny, unless the teasee has openly agreed to relate that way. There is gentle, loving teasing, but in my estimation—as a former teasee—about 98 percent of the time teasing is hurtful.

No matter how old we are, we all have sensitive areas through which insidious sentences can penetrate to our subconscious minds. We are all especially vulnerable to certain types of suggestion. For example, I once discovered a seed sentence I'd been carrying around since childhood: "Women are not happy." No one had told me that, but as a little girl I felt it was true. Some of the women I knew didn't seem very happy. They sighed and complained, and to me that meant unhappiness. As I grew up, I collected data that supported my underlying belief that women weren't happy. One of my mother's favorite laments, uttered with a sigh, was "A man may work from sun to sun, but a woman's work is never done." She may not have been seriously complaining, but as an impressionable child I asked myself, "How can women be happy if they have to work all the time?" Another weed seed for unhappiness

Perhaps predictably, my first marriage was unhappy, and only gradually did I realize that my unhappiness had preceded my marriage. I was uncomfortable when I felt happy. Whenever I felt myself becoming happy, I'd get scared because I felt somehow off balance. So I'd pick a fight, become moody, or sabotage a pleasant situation. Unhappiness was my unconscious comfort zone. Being unhappy kept me congruent with my underlying belief that women were not happy.

As I became aware of my self-defeating underlying belief, I started to work on changing it. Bit by bit, I gave myself permission to be happy. Every time I spotted the old pattern of happiness-sabotage, I stopped and reassured myself that it was okay to feel this good. I replaced my weed sentences with "I have the right to be happy" and "It is okay to feel great!" I'm now very comfortable with happiness, and I've invented some new seed sentences to affirm this new awareness: "Women deserve to be happy and have fun" and "I deserve to be happy and have fun!"

We gravitate toward the familiar and shun the unknown. When we go against our seed sentences, we feel a loss of integrity with ourselves. We don't trust what is outside of our experience. My experience had been that the women I knew weren't happy. That doesn't mean it was necessarily true of the grown-ups I observed, only that I perceived it to be true. Pulling the negative weed sentence from my subconscious has helped me to be who I really am—a fundamentally happy woman.

In the midst of a pleasant afternoon with her brother and his family, Lily found herself becoming depressed for no apparent reason. As she traced the thread of her thoughts, she discovered a seed sentence working in the background: "All good things must come to an end." She had begun to grieve over her relatives' departure hours before the time had come. Her seed sentence was conditioning her to be wary of loss. She couldn't enjoy the moment because of its foreshadowed ending.

Pulling our emotional weeds is important because internalized seed sentences such as, "If I'm rejected, I'll die," sound dramatic and grandiose, but our inner, not-okay child actually perceives rejection as life threatening. When we become aware of such debilitating seed sentences, we can start cleaning our mental closets and replace them with optimistic, healing thoughts. Positive thoughts help us become consciously self-directed rather than unconsciously controlled. Becoming aware of our crippling and fear-provoking weed sentences and replacing them with liberating and affirming flower sentences leads us to the emotional independence of making our own decisions based on what is right for us rather than on what we fear. And that's a lot of what being ourselves is all about.

Thankfully, a huge weed that is slowly being replaced in the spiritual garden is the idea of God/Source as only masculine. As we embrace the mystery that God includes, encompasses, and transcends each gender's qualities, we will be on the way to healing the profound wounds inflicted upon ourselves and our society by thinking otherwise.

While many of us can look back at our early patriarchal religious affiliations with great warmth and feel that they gave us security, love, and the encouragement to become our best selves, others aren't so fortunate. What we heard in church was "Lord, forgive me a miserable sinner." In many organized religions, guilt and sin are bedrock concepts. All men(!)—women didn't even rate a reprimand—were born sinners, and if you sin, you'll suffer anything from eternal roasting in a molten lake of fire to many lifetimes of atonement for the bad karma you've incurred.

The word "sin" is actually an archery term that means "to miss the mark"—a far more kindly interpretation than it's given by many religious institutions. In fact, few denominations are satisfied with the Bible's definitions of sin (in the Ten Commandments, for example). Religious leaders often feel duty bound to create new sins. Not long that ago a woman who showed her ankles was a Jezebel. A girl who smoked was a scarlet woman. But, as women regain their voices and institutions are forced to become more open-minded due to indisputable archeological finds, even Mary Magdalene's reputation as a prostitute is being openly acknowledged as a fabrication of the early church fathers.

It pays to sort through the seed sentences you've carried over from your associations with religion and society. A remarkable number of my clients come from backgrounds of guilt-fostering religious environments. Guilt and fear keep them emotionally vulnerable and prevent them from experiencing their authentic selves.

Lynn is a successful businesswoman, a single mother, respected and loved in her community. She spent her childhood in strict, church-run schools where obeying the rules was the paramount requirement. She never disobeyed, but she also never felt okay about herself, no matter how much outward approval she won. In therapy she had a vivid and excruciating recollection of a severe teacher telling her, "You never get it right!" Lynn, a sensitive child, internalized that thought until it became her default position, one of her basic beliefs about herself, underscored by the seed sentence: "I never do it right." As an adult, even though she more often than not *did* do it right, she never *felt* like a person who did things correctly.

Spirituality is probably the most important aspect of ourselves that we humans need to explore and expand, but I don't think we can experience our authentic spiritual selves until we have revamped the unquestioned, self-condemning beliefs we've acquired in our contact with society and some religions.

Many of our semiconscious seed sentences express fear of offending others. The trouble is, our freedom diminishes if we are afraid of standing up to others. I'm not advocating unkindness or discourtesy since it's very important for our own self-esteem to think empathetically of others. But craving others' approval in order to feel okay about ourselves kills creativity and authenticity.

Women have a tendency to shackle themselves to others' moods. What happens when your husband, boss, or kids are in a foul mood and nothing pleases them? Do you dance around like a trained bear, trying to make them laugh and be happy? I used to do that, because I always felt that I was somehow to blame for other people's bad moods. When they were rejecting, I felt I was less of a person. Their rejection was unbearable, and so I tried to dance to whatever tune they were inaudibly playing. It never worked, and I became increasingly angry with myself for behaving like a wind-up Prozac pill.

Part of gaining emotional strength has been learning to adopt as my own seed sentence the title of an excellent book by Laura Huxley, *I Am Not the Target.* I've become better at stepping back from situations when I feel someone is projecting their negative feelings onto me. In the presence of angry or rejecting vibrations, my stomach still knots up, my throat closes, and I want to run to the nearest cookie jar for solace, but I say to my body and my internal little girl: "We're okay. I will keep you safe." With reassurance from these powerful new seed sentences, my fear dissipates and I end up feeling proud of myself. A threatening situation is transformed into a pleasant inner victory; another bout of fear is positively overcome without my falling into the dependence trap.

The following is a list of common weed sentences and nicknames, which can easily turn into seed sentences. What seed sentences did you gather as you grew up? List them in the space provided. Look at your seed sentences and begin to negate their power with your awareness. As you replace weed sentences with flowers, you'll be freed from their stranglehold on your behavior. Are your seed sentences roses, lilies, and jonquils—or pyracantha, poison ivy, and stinkweed?

You can pull up your weed thoughts and replace them with thought flowers that will blossom into a beautiful life.

Weed Sentences

1. I should have been a boy.

2. Tears are a form of self-pity.

3. You have to give sex in order to get love.

4. Nice girls do more than their share.

5. Women are not happy.

6. I am responsible for another person's happiness.

7. Women/men can't be trusted.

8. It's a cruel world out there.

9. Women over forty aren't attractive.

10. I'm ugly, unlovable, (_____), or (_____).

11. I can't...

12. Don't air your dirty laundry in public.

13. I've always got to be "up."

14. Nothing I do is good enough.

15. That's men's work (or that's women's work).

16. The children are totally my responsibility.

17. My sister (lover, brother, father, dog) is better than I am.

18. Life is hard and then you die.

Your Own Weed Sentences

1. _____

2. _____

3. _____

4. _____

5. _____

6. _____

Nicknames

1. Chubby Cheeks

2. Lardo

3. Fatty Patty

4. Stick

5. Freckles

6. Sappy Sue

7. Four Eyes

8. Thunder Thighs

9. Bucky

10. Baby

11. Betty Boob

12. Schnoz

Some of Your Nicknames

1. _____

2. _____

3. _____

4. _____

Freeing ourselves from underlying assumptions and bringing our beliefs into harmony with the goal of lovingly supporting ourselves takes time and doesn't come easily. We need to be gentle with ourselves and remember that we are called upon to love our neighbors as ourselves, not to the exclusion of ourselves. As a natural outgrowth of loving ourselves, we will learn to love others more fully and authentically.

Become aware of your beliefs and automatic default settings. Bring them into the light of your present, adult knowledge. Gently acknowledge that they are what they are. Then accept that they constitute what you've believed until now, and that you can transform them into beliefs that allow you to fully express who you really are. Without judgment, patiently begin working to change subconscious and limiting beliefs into true expressions of your authentic self.

CHAPTER TEN

DROWNING IN LIFE'S DEBRIS

Anxiety is love's greatest killer, because it is
like the stranglehold of the drowning.

ANAÏS NIN

None of us is completely free of inner debris. We've all grieved. We all carry around unresolved emotional junk. We've all been stressed out and have suppressed anger, guilt, and resentment. We're human, and these experiences help us to grow. But we can only grow and be who we really are by healing our inner hurts, sharing our pain, and forgiving ourselves and others. If we leave piles of unresolved emotional debris under the rug, there's always the danger that we may stumble over them and fall right into the crater of emotional dependence.

It's true that growth involves risk, but if you increase your ability to tolerate pain, you'll be able to risk acting even when you're afraid, which means that you will be in the process of developing emotional strength and higher self-esteem. As you clean the debris out from under your inner carpet, you'll feel an increasing sense of freedom and independence. Not immediately, perhaps, because it takes time for the healing process to gain force and momentum, but if you work at it consistently and with patience, healing will begin and creativity will start to flow.

STRESSED AND DISTRESSED

Probably one of the weightiest albatross hanging around our necks is stress. In these days of downsizing, multitasking, single motherhood, credit card debt, and soaring prices, who among us has not felt the burden of stress?

According to the International Labor Office/Bureau of Labor Statistics, Americans work an average of 1,966 hours per year, which is more than workers in Japan, Britain, France, and Germany. In addition, the number of American workers, especially women, who put in more than 50 or 60 hours per week has been rising. In light of these figures, Chicago labor lawyer Thomas Geoghegan says, "I know there are people who claim that working exhausting hours is part of the culture—a way to achieve self-actualization. Only why does it feel like self-vaporization?"

It's important to note that these statistics relate to on-the-job hours and don't take into consideration the intensive in-the-home and with-the-family ones women put in. Whew! Is it any wonder we suffer from *Zerrisenheit*, a German word meaning "torn-to-pieces-hood"?

Of course, some stress is unavoidable and can be de-stressed by the way we think about it and refer to it. By changing our beliefs and attitudes, much of the tension and anxiety can be drained from tasks that need to be done.

I remember when all four of our kids were living at home and eating heartily, I went through a stressed-out and resentful period because I was the only cook in the house. Everyone was perfectly capable of foraging for themselves, but too many foraged meals activated my Bad-Mother-Button.

Responding to my umpteenth complaint about cooking, a friend asked, "Are you going to continue to do the cooking?" I answered yes and she said, "Then you have two choices. You can cook meals as gifts spiced with love or you can cook them as obligations poisoned with resentment." Hmm.... It took many self-reminders but, eventually, my attitude shifted and I could (mostly) cook with love.

But stress is not simply a product of outside circumstances. According to Norm Shealy, M.D., Ph.D., founder of the American Holistic Medical Association, the root cause of stress is lack of self-esteem and the inability to forgive. A majority of the twenty thousand patients Dr. Shealy has treated suffer from chronic pain. From talking with and caring for those patients, he concluded, "These people are broken-hearted because they feel they can't meet others' expectations and thereby can't love themselves." The most successful therapeutic intervention at Shealy Institute in Springfield, Missouri, is "total immersion in nurturing for two solid weeks," says Shealy.

Intrigued by Dr. Shealy's premise, I looked up self-esteem and self-love in my *Webster's Third New International Dictionary.* Guess what? The only synonym given for both terms is "conceit." Is it any wonder we find it difficult to give ourselves permission to have self-esteem and practice self-love?

In exploring the following exercise, it's important to remember that needed changes can be inner, outer, or both.

Identifying Stressors

1. What are the greatest stressors in my life?

    _____

    _____

    _____

2. What am I doing about them?

    _____

    _____

    _____

3. How is that working?

    _____

    _____

    _____

4. What might work better?

    _____

    _____

    _____

5. What small steps can I take today to decrease stress?

_____

_____

_____

While the scientific among you may scoff, I want to share a stress reducer that I find very helpful. My friends and I call it "thumping thymus therapy." Holistic health advocates have found that stimulating the thymus gland by firmly tapping on it three or four times daily reduces the effects of stress both physically and emotionally. It is believed that thumping the thymus triggers the release of revitalizing hormones that enhance our life-force.

Sure, I've read the medical literature that states the thymus gland has atrophied in the adult human, but I also thump regularly and, in times of stress and grief, feel it really does minimize my distress and facilitates healing.

The thymus is located in the center of your chest a tiny tad above heart level. So, what the heck. Try it if you want and, if it works for you as it does for me and many others, who cares if the AMA chortles?

An added bonus for me is if I'm thumping away in the presence of my husband, who is also a thymus thumper, he knows something is bothering me and often asks what it is. No other clue as been as easy for him to pick up.

GUILT

Guilt: the gift that keeps on giving.

ERMA BOMBECK

Erma was right. Among other things, guilt keeps on giving us ulcers, regrets, anxiety, stress, and self-doubt. And it takes away our vitality, creativity, strength, and worst of all, our ability to truly love.

One of the biggest stressors and highest mounds swept under our emotional carpet is guilt. Even among successful and liberated women, guilt spreads with the rampant fury of a wildfire. We feel guilty if our kids don't turn out as we think they should, as our parents think they should, or as society thinks they should. I know a woman whose son was an all-around superstar in high school. In college, he burned out and left school. He didn't work much, and when he did, it was always in menial jobs. Her cry: "Where did I go wrong?"

Women Feel Guilty If They

DO	DON'T
Work	Work
Discipline the children	Discipline the children
Make more money than their husbands or fathers	Bring in "their share"

Take time for personal interests	Take time for personal interests
Get divorced	Have a happy marriage
Want free time and/ or solitude	Nurture the spiritual side of their nature
Chat on the phone	Keep up their friendships
Say no	Say no
Have sex or want it	Have sex or want it
Get sick	Keep their bodies youthful and fit
Get angry	Stand up for themselves
Have children	Have children

Do you see yourself on that list? I do. I used to feel guilty if the cat had matted fur. Who said it was my responsibility to de-mat the cat? I did, of course.

We've been led to believe that we're responsible for others' happiness, success, moods, arguments, and failures. When our families aren't happy, it's our fault.

According to Lynne Caine, author of *What Did I Do Wrong? Mothers, Children, Guilt*, Sigmund Freud helped perpetuate this belief. In an interview, she said:

> Our society is saturated with mother-blaming. This began, I believe, in the 1940s. That's when the

popularizers of Freudian psychology discovered mothers were to blame for everything that went wrong with the American family. In 1942, Philip Wylie wrote Generation of Vipers, in which he proclaimed that Mom was a jerk. He coined the term "momism." From then on it's been open season on mothers. Mother-blaming—and in some cases mother-hating—abounds in our literature, movies, and on TV. Mothers, stepmothers, and mother-in-laws are portrayed as being either manipulative, possessive, controlling, and bitchy, or as being wimpy, ineffectual and ludicrous.

This idea has become part of our belief system. For most of us, it's an underlying assumption—something we've swallowed whole. We create "momist" seed sentences, such as "If my child, husband, or friend isn't happy, it's my fault. I need to fix my husband's life. I'm responsible for my child's successes in college."

Exaggerated affirmations of responsibility like these are loaded with guilt-producing power that keep us emotionally beholden to those who, in truth, are responsible for and to themselves. In fact, we can never *make* people happy or successful.

Years ago my husband and I took a magazine quiz to see if we were compatible. One of the questions was "When you and your spouse argue, is it sometimes/usually/always his/her fault?" My answer was "sometimes" and his was "always." He believed the myth that I was responsible for his happiness. Arguing made him unhappy, therefore if we argued, it must be my fault.

RESPONSIBILITY SPONGE

If our internal dialogue chants "If I am only nice enough, kind enough, patient enough, everything/everyone will be okay," we are Responsibility Sponges who assume responsibility for other people's happiness. Responsibility Sponges are everyone's designated garbage cans wearing signs that tell our mates, children, parents, and employers: "Dump here."

There was a time when, if there was a puddle of unhappiness around one of my kids or my husband, I was quick to leap in and try to mop it up. After two husbands and four kids, my sponge became extremely soggy. I believed that somehow I had failed them or offended them if they were unhappy. I felt it was part of my job as wife, mother, and human being never to offend anybody. But then I discovered that *our freedom diminishes if we are afraid of standing up to others.*

I truly believed it was my role to carry everyone's garbage and mop up all their puddles. If I didn't, I felt guilty. If I did and they didn't "get happy," I felt guilty and resentful. The role of Responsibility Sponge carries with it the need to teach others what they don't know, especially about feelings. As a therapist, I was definitely subject to that delusion. I knew all about feelings. But my husband hated my preaching and felt like I was trying to be both mother and guru: two roles that can play havoc with your love life.

While we do need loving relationships, we never need to turn our lives over to someone else or take over responsibility for another person's life. By putting our happiness in others' hands, we become dependent; by taking responsibility for others' happiness, we invite them to become dependent—an invitation that a healthy human spirit will vigorously refuse.

APPROPRIATE AND INAPPROPRIATE GUILT

Guilt is either appropriate or inappropriate. Appropriate guilt is a compass that tells you when you're going in the wrong direction. Like a road sign, it looms ahead saying, "Stop. Wrong way." Appropriate guilt is there to help. Acknowledge it and it subsides; its job is done. For instance, if you make a thoughtless or hurtful remark, a twinge of guilt can be an indicator that you need to apologize.

Naturally there's also appropriate guilt that's deep, long-lasting, and painful. That kind of intensive, appropriate guilt signals a severe deviation from acceptable behavior and the need for a very radical examination of your life. We hope a murderer or child abuser would sooner or later feel that kind of remorse.

Inappropriate guilt is Erma's type of guilt. It hangs on forever and paralyzes us with "I'm wrongs", "if onlys", and "what ifs". A friend told me, "I have a round-trip ticket on the guilt train. Anytime it rolls through the station, I climb aboard!" Another friend quipped, "I never get off—station or not!"

WHERE DO WE GET ON THE GUILT TRAIN?

Children are keenly attuned to the emotional vibrations of their parents and other adults. They are exquisitely sensitive barometers of family feelings. From birth to the age of six or seven, children are not merely sensitive but also very self-centered. Therefore, whenever something happens in the home, in their minds, they caused it. When my oldest son was five years old he said to me, "Mommy, please don't cry. When you cry, I feel like I've killed someone."

I knew how my son felt because as a little girl, I wore French braids and every morning, as my mother did my hair, she sighed repeatedly. Times were tough: my father was away at war, money was tight, my mother had to work, and I was left in the care of an unloving grandmother. To my little heart and mind, each of those sighs and the feelings behind them meant I was a burden. *I* was making my mother unhappy. A generation later my son felt that the tears I was shedding over his dad and my divorce were his fault.

Through much of my adult life, it upset me terribly whenever anyone sighed. I immediately felt guilty and had a tremendous urge to console them or to run away. Telling myself how silly that was brought no relief until I realized that the roots of my underlying assumption lay in those early hair-braiding sessions with my mother. As a child, I had lacked the awareness and sophistication to simply ask Mother if it bothered her to braid my hair. I could only take clues and fit them into my child's narrow reality. My underlying assumption became "I'm a burden. I need to make other people happy, because it's my fault if they're not."

We get off the guilt train by reminding ourselves that we are not responsible for other people's happiness.

It took me a long time to convince my guilt-prone inner child that she really didn't need to punish herself with inappropriate guilt feelings. With gentle, patient, persistent reminders, she came around to believing me. Now, she's better at relaxing and letting others carry their own responsibilities. Every time something happens that would have made me feel guilty in the past, and I don't regress, I feel exhilarated and free.

Talking to others about our feelings is very helpful in resolving guilt. It's amazing how quickly guilt can melt away when we receive loving feedback from other people who can be more objective about what's happening to us because they're not emotionally involved.

The last time I saw the friend who'd said she had a round-trip ticket on the guilt train, she told me she no longer felt guilty.

I was intrigued and sent her a card with a picture of a bewildered little figure carrying a suitcase. It said: "I'm going on a guilt trip. Would you mind dropping by to feed my paranoia?" Her response was: "I don't mind feeding your paranoia anytime— since I stopped feeding (or feeding on) my own guilt, I have more time for such good deeds." She had made a conscious decision to stop feeling guilty, and she succeeded. So can you.

ANGER AND RESENTMENT

Scratch a woman and you find a rage.

VIRGINIA WOOLF

Another pile of dirt that gets swept under our emotional carpet consists of anger and resentment. For women, anger is the ultimate taboo. We are taught not to be angry, and if we are, to definitely not express it. We learn to mask our anger, to express it in covert ways, or to dutifully hold it in until all hell breaks loose.

Conclusive stress research has established that suppressed or inappropriately expressed anger comes out in many forms, including withdrawal, ulcerated colons, migraines, child abuse, depression, and suicide.

Patricia Sun, a teacher of spirituality and conscious living, says, "Anger is our intuitive, right brain telling us, 'Whoops, something's not right here!'" Anger is a warning device. To resolve it wisely, first pay attention to it, keeping in mind that you can choose not to act out any of the things your emotionally charged feelings suggest to you. Then ask what "whoops" your anger is trying to alert you to. Anger, if not allowed to fester and grow out of proportion, is healthy, like a smoke alarm that if heeded can prevent all sorts of damage.

We ignore our anger primarily because we don't want to rock the boat. Of course, there are usually more specific reasons: we've been punished for being angry, we've been rejected for not acting nice, and so on. When our conditioning prevails, anger smolders into resentment. Resentment becomes an out-of-control, insidious force, which casts blame on others.

Rebecca was married to the same man for almost fifty years. She was angry many times but only rarely expressed her feelings. When she and her husband established their patterns of married behavior, assertiveness wasn't popular. Whenever she tried to express her anger, her husband reacted with one caustic verbal blast and then withdrew into icy silence that lasted for days or even weeks.

Rebecca was no dummy. She learned not to say what she was feeling. But her unexpressed anger turned into smoldering resentment, which expressed itself as accidents, ulcers, loss of interest in sex, and finally fatal cancer. Rebecca died blaming herself for allowing her fear of her husband's responses to curtail her ability to express her feelings.

Because of increased psychological understanding, we're more cognizant now that it's okay to be angry and that it's natural to express our anger. We have a right to be angry, but with that right comes a responsibility to express our anger constructively. If you express your anger in destructive ways, you set yourself up to feel guilty and create more debris instead of removing some. In this case, *constructive* means "not destructive."

Not expressing your anger is unhealthy. Some of us are better than others at keeping the lid on, but sooner or later we blow it. I like the image of a pressure cooker: the pressure builds up and the food inside gets cooked quickly, but if you don't remember to open the little valve on top so the steam can escape in a controlled manner, stand back 'cause dinner's gonna be all over the ceiling.

Once you've allowed pressure to build up to the point where it can only blow, you can't express yourself constructively. So, once again, the trick is to become aware of your anger and resentment. There it is, whether you want it or not, and it's trying to tell you something. Acknowledge your feelings to someone who can help you sort through them. It doesn't have to be the person with whom you're upset. In fact, sometimes that's exactly the wrong person to talk to because, in the heat of the moment, you may say something that will cause lasting damage—or the person you're talking to may be the kind who can't listen. Now accept that you have a right to your anger and know that it's there to guide you. If you express your anger constructively, you won't need to experience resentment or guilt.

Anger can become a valuable tool when you learn to express it well. Step back from the feelings a bit and ask yourself what you want to accomplish with your anger. Do you want to reconnect with a person? Right a wrong? Understand a situation better? Be understood? Free yourself from a harmful relationship?

It's never helpful to hurt or abuse a person physically or emotionally under the influence of anger (or at any other time). But there are constructive ways to release pent-up anger. When you're steaming, it's a good idea to release the unmanageable excess anger before you confront the person with whom you're angry. No one reacts positively to a full-face blast from the dragon's fiery jaws. An angry frontal attack puts even the most invulnerable person on the defensive.

I like to beat beds with a tennis racket, especially the bed of the person I'm angry with (when they're not in it, of course, and preferably not even home). I know women who go out driving on the freeway and scream or who throw eggs at trees. These methods may sound a little weird, but they work (and are lots of fun for those of us who've spent a lifetime trying to be nice girls)! Anger creates steam, and it's only constructive to release it one manageable puff at a time so that nobody gets scalded.

Carol releases her anger in a way that helps her local charities. She goes to a thrift store, buys a bunch of old china, goes to the dump and throws plates, cups, and saucers as far and as hard as she can. The dump is a great place for her crockery-smashing sessions, because she doesn't feel guilty about making a mess and she doesn't have to clean up afterward. Her teenage daughter likes to go with her. Carol has been able to give herself and her daughter permission to have anger toward her ex-husband, who deserted them, and to express that anger constructively. She and her daughter usually end up laughing together, a wonderfully healing conclusion.

It isn't appropriate to voice your feelings to the people concerned if you think that you'll come away the loser, you won't be heard, you'll damage a relationship beyond repair, or you'll jeopardize your job. In such cases, it's wiser to choose not to talk to the person.

Years ago when I was going through my divorce and my whole life was up for review, I went through a period of feeling intense anger toward my parents. Fortunately I chose not to share my feelings with them but rather to release them in other ways, like poison-pen letters that were never sent and talking with other people. Why was that fortunate? Because as I became clear about the source of my anger, I found it didn't have that much to do with my parents. Sure, I'd had my share of hurts in childhood—we all have. But if I had projected my anger onto my parents, I would have hurt them terribly and might even have fractured our relationship irreparably. They didn't deserve to be made the targets for all the rage and frustration I was feeling over my divorce and the events that had led up to it. However, I did choose understanding friends with whom to share my rage.

If suppressed, repressed, or destructively expressed, anger, like a gun turned against the holder, can cripple us. If used constructively, it can be very empowering. Outrage only harms us when it becomes *in*rage.

UNRESOLVED GRIEF

Grief is a process. If it is allowed, healing
will take place naturally.

HOSPICE OF THE FOOTHILLS

No matter how rich our life or how bright our future, we all experience grief. To live is to change and be vulnerable to loss. Loss brings grief. Unresolved grief takes so much strength to suppress that we have little energy left over for other things— like being our authentic selves. Adopting new patterns of behavior and attitudes happens best when we are not burdened with the debris of unresolved grief. Carrying old grief keeps us in a reaction rut rather than an action mode.

Since none of us escapes grief, it is important we learn healthy ways to grieve. Natural grieving is allowing ourselves to experience our feelings and move through them at the time of loss. This process is cleansing and leads to full recovery. Often an enhancement of spirituality and compassion is our reward.

Unresolved grief is created when we don't allow ourselves to work through feelings as they arise. If we deny having painful feelings or put them on a shelf, they don't simply evaporate. Rather, unresolved feelings gnaw at our energy, prey on our emotions, and generally debilitate us.

Grief comes in many forms. Grief over death and loss is just one. Another is grief over the things we feel we should have done or shouldn't have done. When we fight with a friend or mate, we grieve. When too many bills pile up and money is tight, we grieve. Allowing ourselves to get so busy we can't enjoy life is a pervasive grief for those of us who need to "do it all." Anything unfinished and left to fester becomes emotional litter.

Many of us allow emotional debris to collect in our hearts, minds, and souls. Soon the mounds of debris that we've created become too big to ignore. They keep us from walking around freely in our own inner homes and separate us from those we care about. Emotional debris erodes our freedom to make conscious choices about who we are and how we want to be in the world.

In order to heal and become your authentic self you must recognize and unravel the pain of grief. When the pain of grief winds itself around your heart, don't try to "pull yourself up by your bootstraps" and tough it out. You will only accumulate debris by refusing to face your pain honestly and courageously.

Talk. Share your pain. Cry over it. Read about loss and grieving, join a group, and be especially careful of your body, which is weaker and more vulnerable when you are grieving. Pace yourself to recovery. Don't try to do business as usual. Realize, while you are healing from a loss, that you've been hit by an emotional truck or, if it's a small loss, by a VW Bug. You may need to grieve for five minutes, five weeks, or in diminishing intensity, for several years. But time is a healer, and though it may hardly seem possible while you grieve, if you allow yourself to move through grief, you will heal.

It's true that we're never the same after a severe loss, but we can heal and even become kinder and gentler as a result of the grieving process.

ISOLATION

As I begin to understand each of my clients more deeply, I hear a silent plea echoing behind their spoken words of pain: "See me, hear me, hold me." All of us need the close contact and validation of our fellow humans. Women are social beings who thrive on connection. When we don't experience such intimacy, we feel isolated and unfulfilled.

As a therapist, I see the ravages of isolation daily. People who've been unable to share their concerns with understanding friends or families feel a chronic isolation that gathers like huge piles of unresolved emotional debris and turns eventually into life-threatening despair.

A certain amount of solitude is essential. Isolation is something entirely different. We need to feel we are a part of the groups with which we live and work, to feel attached to them, and to identify with them in a grounded, mutually helpful, complementary way. Churches, families, schools, self-help groups, and friends all help us overcome feelings of isolation.

Many of us began to feel isolated early in life. If the adults who cared for us misunderstood, criticized, teased, or judged us, we began to fear sharing ourselves with others. The world felt unsafe. When they didn't see, hear, or hold us, or if they loved us only when we were doing things right, we began to feel that even if it were safe to share our real feelings, we weren't worthy to do so. We became adults who didn't want to burden others with our troubles or air our dirty laundry in public. But we pay dearly for our silence. Isolation is a form of emotional suicide.

People in the bereavement groups I lead are astounded by how much better they feel once they share their pain with others and learn that they are not alone or unique in their reactions. Their isolation is broken, connections form, and healing begins.

Frequently in our isolation we feel unaccepted and unacceptable. We think we're different, the only ones who feel a certain way. Everyone else looks squared-away and happy. We're the weird ones. We develop a socially suitable facade behind which we hide our true feelings. We become social chameleons, changing to suit different situations and people. To some extent, all of us do this when we feel frightened about revealing how vulnerable we are in certain situations.

Dr. Pauline Rose Clance, in her book *The Imposter Phenomenon: Overcoming the Fear that Haunts Your Success*, shows that none of us have a flawless self-concept. She writes: "I constantly see men and women (especially women) who have every right to be on top of the world, but instead they're miserable because in their eyes they never measure up. They feel fraudulent."

No matter how successful we are, or how loved, many of us hear an incessant, convincing voice inside that reminds us of our faults and failings. The way to transform that inner saboteur is to learn to love and accept ourselves as we are. We need to come to an understanding of the part of us that is judgmental and tries so terribly hard to be perfect. Madame Marie Curie said, "Nothing in life is to be feared. It is only to be understood." In our confusion, we fear that our faults and weaknesses are unforgivable, so we isolate ourselves behind a mask and never move beyond it into the freedom of understanding. No wonder we have difficulty being ourselves.

Breaking out of isolation takes courage. If your isolation is a long-standing habit, give yourself permission to go slowly and safely. Remind yourself that you carry around an inner child who feels isolation is the only safe way to live. Why is she frightened? Can she count on you to protect her? One of the greatest boons you can give yourself is to become a loving parent to your inner child.

If we aren't gentle and kind to ourselves as we risk change, we merely reinforce the conviction that the world isn't a safe place and therefore we'd better not take the gamble of sharing who we really are.

Explore the reasons why you isolate yourself. What are you protecting? What do you fear? Find people with whom you can take off your mask—people who are willing to see, hear, and hold you. By all means, avoid throwing your (emotional) pearls before swine. Swine are people who say things like "You shouldn't feel that way" or "That's stupid—why don't you just ____?" Swine are very judgmental and, in their own minds, always right. Swine make you wish you'd kept your mouth shut. Be discerning about those with whom you doff your protective facade. You very much need—and deserve—empathetic and kind understanding.

Become loving and honest with yourself too. None of us is perfect. We all have our share of inner squiggly worms (and some boa constrictors). The more we can honestly and gently be vulnerable with ourselves and others, the more we free ourselves from our fears and foibles. The freer we are from fear, the more emotional strength we gain.

Do yourself a transformative favor and find a creative outlet for your pain. One of the best ways to sweep away old fear-debris and break isolation is to reach out in honesty, love, and service to someone else—not because we "should" or as a guilt-induced sacrifice, but as an invitation to a loving bond and a mutual boost to ourselves and to another person.

PART THREE

Healing: Owning Your Own Excellence

∽

CHAPTER ELEVEN

BEYOND FEAR: TRANSFORMING THE DRAGONS

Who knows what women can be when they are
finally free to become themselves? Who knows
what women's intelligence will contribute when
it can be nourished without denying love?

BETTY FRIEDAN

N ow that we have explored many of the ways and reasons why we women get trapped in emotional dependence, let's look at how we can move beyond fear and limiting patterns of behavior. By transforming our inner dragons and owning our own excellence, we become more able to honor ourselves and our process and, as a result, move ever closer to healthy self-esteem and independence.

How do parents encourage the infant who's just learning to walk? They hold her hand, provide a safe environment, and congratulate each new success.

Similarly, in moving beyond fear, realize that you must go forward at a beginner's pace. Take baby steps. Be proud of each faltering toddle, each newly taken footstep. Become a kind and encouraging parent to yourself. Gently congratulate yourself on your successes and comfort yourself after failure.

CULTIVATING SELF-ESTEEM

Self-esteem is a fairly recent concept. We now help our children to develop it and we try to enhance it in ourselves. But when I was growing up, self-esteem was confused with self-centeredness and big-headedness. As a result, we learned to play down our talents for fear of appearing conceited. We often accentuated our shortcomings and acted humble because we thought that's what it took to be well-liked and accepted.

However, if criticism and humility aren't balanced with appreciation for things we do well and our willingness to learn, we can become critical, judgmental, and stress-filled. Self-critical people see their mistakes leaping in front of them festooned with neon lights while their triumphs wither from lack of attention. They look at their real or imagined imperfections through powerful binoculars and then turn the glasses around for a cursory glimpse at their good points and successes. If this is our habit, failures loom large and successes look like specks—mere accidents or "lucky breaks."

I used to shoot poison darts at the positives in myself and caress the negatives. Do you ever dwell painfully on something dumb you've said? I did that all the time. I'd even go back over encounters with people looking for things I'd said wrong. One of my seed sentences was "You always put your foot in your mouth." Mentally I scanned every encounter for the taste of shoe leather.

Until the last several years, it never occurred to me to go back over an encounter and congratulate myself for something I had done or said well. But doing so helps me cultivate self-esteem and the courage to own my own excellence. It's a matter of retraining ourselves to behave like a loving mentor, friend, or parent toward ourselves, encouraging our positive attributes and being gentle with our frailties.

Give yourself permission to know what a fantastic person you are! Learn to **SEE: Savor Excellence Everyday.** Start liking and admiring yourself, loving and nurturing yourself. Become an honest and appreciative mirror for your own reflection.

Self-esteem is quiet and confident; it doesn't need to boast and be self-centered. True self-esteem empowers us to be loving and giving. We needn't fear we'll become selfish if we honor our own excellence. Actually, as we own ours, we do others a favor by encouraging them to accept their excellence as well.

STEPS TOWARD TRANSFORMATION

Become *aware* of the dragons and fears inside you. Nonjudgmentally observing feelings gives us the opportunity to understand ourselves better and allows the feelings themselves to heal and transform. If you fearfully resist feelings, labeling them bad/wrong/ugly, they'll stick to your mind and grow. *Acknowledge* all of your feelings. You don't need to act on them; just see that they are within you. Invite your dragons into the light of your attention and respect. Then, *accept* them. Feelings aren't right or wrong; they just are. A gentle climate of love and acceptance fosters the possibility of change and growth in feelings that only worsen if kept hidden.

Change is action; old habits are reactions. To change both ourselves and our feelings, it's often necessary to consciously choose new actions. All the buried patterns we've talked about so far are ingrained, passive, fixed, change-resisting reactions to people and circumstances. To be free of such reactions we need to heal the feelings that motivate them and create fresh, new actions to replace them. We need to act rather than react. Breaking reaction cycles goes a long way toward freeing ourselves to own our own excellence and be who we are meant to be.

BECOME AWARE, PAUSE, CHOOSE

STEP 1: BECOME AWARE

Bring into the open limiting patterns, reactions, and/or fears. Understanding follows awareness.

STEP 2: PAUSE

Before you act, step back and take time out. Breathe deeply and regularly in order to center yourself. To gain perspective, it's important to put distance between yourself and your automatic reactions. We can't see much with our noses pressed right up against what it is we're examining. Explore your feelings and compare your options for responding to them. Remember how you have reacted in the past. Is that behavior appropriate now, or would you rather choose other conscious, creative, more healing action?

STEP 3: CHOOSE

This step is crucial. By pausing, you've taken yourself off automatic pilot and are now free to decide on a new course of action. How would you like to act? If the old reaction isn't working, you have the capacity to choose to act in a different way. You do not have to continue old patterns. We are the designated drivers on our individual life's highway.

If you take a single word out of this book and make it your own on a day-to-day basis, I hope it's *choose*. Being able to choose to act differently, even while feeling the old way, may be the most liberating growth you can accomplish.

Once when my husband and I were having a confrontation in which I felt judged and rejected, I recognized an old reaction pattern, a three-phase dance I used to go into whenever I felt threatened. First, I'd feel guilty and wrong for "making" him unhappy, so I'd become jovial and conciliatory in order to jolly him out of his mood. Second, when that didn't work, I became the counselor-in-residence and (oh, so calmly) pointed out the error of his ways, reasonably citing the various psychological reasons for the misunderstanding. That never worked. No one, especially our mate, is very receptive to being "enlightened" concerning the reasons for his or her irrational behavior, especially while they're in the midst of feeling hurt, angry, or righteous.

When neither of those tactics worked, I became frustrated, lonely, and discouraged. I then moved into the third phase in which I withdrew and slogged around in a cloud of resentment and disappointment. Obviously my mood was his fault. Why couldn't he be different? Plop! I'd fallen into my victim role.

During this particular episode, before the familiar pattern got into full swing, I paused and asked myself some very important questions:

1. Have these reactions worked in the past?

2. Do I feel better when I react in these ways?

3. Is our relationship better after I've danced in my clown tutu or donned my counselor cape?

In each case, the answer was a resounding "No." So the next question was obvious:

4.   Do I still want to react this way?

Now, having paused and stepped back from my feelings, I could choose how I would act.

I decided to detach myself. I withdrew from the conflict between us, not in anger, resentment, or with a feeling of rejection, but in order to allow him the space and time to take responsibility for his own feelings if he chose to.

I sequestered myself with my tape recorder, cried some cleansing tears, wrote in my journal, and made some notes for this book. Instead of trying to convince my husband to change, I changed. I stepped out of the victim role, gave up being a Responsibility Sponge, and took care of myself.

From the neck up, I was exhilarated by the change in my behavior, but my body continued to behave in the old way. My stomach churned and a giant talon seized my throat. In my body the feelings of guilt, rejection, fear, and loneliness continued to run rampant.

I talked to my body and to my sad and lonely inner child, telling them that I would take care of them. I encouraged myself to relax and kept assuring myself that I was safe and that I no longer needed the old feelings to protect me. Very slowly, my body began to get the message. After a few hours, the exhilaration in my head percolated through my entire body and I felt great!

I had been true to myself, taken charge of my reactions, and turned an old dragon into a new and better way of relating to my husband. It was a very freeing experience for me and also better for him since the old trying-to-make-it-better pattern had always created resentment and hostility toward him. My new pattern of action freed us both from having to deal with that.

LIVING AND LOVING
FROM OVERFLOW

An important part of owning our own excellence is nourishing ourselves and others, and doing so in the best way possible: by giving love and support rather than bartering it. Paradoxically, as we truly commit to ourselves, it becomes easier and easier to love others from a sense of overflow rather than obligation. Loving from overflow allows us to base our relationships on complementary interdependence rather than dependence and a sense of burdened responsibility. As complementary partners, we can then work and play together toward the good of our relationships, family, and the greater whole, free from the tyranny of fear and depletion.

A vessel filled and spilling over can give with no hint of martyrdom. A chalice that is full to the brim and overflowing doesn't care who or what receives its excess because it has all it can hold already. The same is true for us. We nurture best from overflow.

Take a moment to imagine yourself as an exquisite chalice. How full are you right now? Overflowing, half full, flirting with empty, drained dry? One of the best ways to fill our personal chalice is to nurture and nourish all parts of ourselves.

To help you ascertain how full your life's chalice is, please use the following illustration:

DAY	1	2	3	4	5	6	7
PHYSICAL							
EMOTIONAL							
MENTAL							
SPIRITUAL							

Review the four quadrants of your being: physical, emotional, mental, and spiritual. Do you have something going for you in each of these areas, or have you become imbalanced? Every day note what you've done for yourself in each of the four areas. Make a commitment to yourself to give time and attention to those areas that need more than you are currently giving. By filling your chalice and balancing your life, you love and nourish yourself and also have more to give others.

PHYSICAL QUADRANT

Is your body fit and healthy? Do you treat it with appreciative respect? It's important to get at least twenty to thirty minutes of aerobic exercise three times a week; even more is better—a brisk walk at lunchtime will do more for us in the long run than the quick-energy infusion of a handful of Hershey kisses. Strength training is excellent for women. It decreases our chances of having osteoporosis and increases our sense of emotional well-being. You don't have to join a gym to lift weights either. At home, you can lift sacks of flour or canned goods and do push-ups, etc. With a little creativity, creating a good home workout is possible.

Really being disciplined about exercise is probably one of hardest things for most of us, but don't let yourself sabotage your good intentions by excuses such as you don't have time or you look lumpy in tights. It is amazing how much difference a fit body makes in how confident and capable we feel. Give your body good food and plenty of replenishing rest. You cannot run (and most of us do, indeed, run) without effective fuel and restorative periods for refueling. You are your body's only maintenance engineer—it counts on you.

EMOTIONAL QUADRANT

Everything we've discussed so far is actually designed to increase your emotional health. But besides learning to truly be yourself, what feeds you emotionally? Probably anything that increases your enthusiasm, zest for life, and feelings of loving and being loved. Whether it's by way of intimate conversations with mates, friends, and children, a job well done, an artistic outlet, or heartfelt laughter, your emotions need nourishment. Need a good cry? Well, why not? Want a raise? Ask.

Listen to your inner signals and you will know when you need emotional energy, and then find a positive source to fill your need. If talking to friends fills you emotionally, make sure that you give yourself the gift of connecting with them regularly. We are all different, and only we know what best fills the emotional quadrant of our life chalice. As we give ourselves permission to fill up and overflow emotionally, we are also infused with greater enthusiasm. Life becomes more joyous, fun, and spontaneous.

MENTAL QUADRANT

Just as the body and emotions need regular exercise and good food, the mind also craves the kind of nourishment it can get from fulfilling work, challenging ideas, books, conversation, and many other sources. Is your brain too idle? Is your day repetitive, predictable, and not mentally stimulating? Do you catch yourself talking "little kid" talk? Do you often "veg out," exhausted, in front of the television? In order to give up being drugged by TV or dulling habits, we can take a class, read a good book, work a crossword puzzle, explore job possibilities, or learn a sport. Our brains can be great allies in gaining emotional strength and enhancing self-esteem but, to do so, they need exercise.

SPIRITUAL QUADRANT

We are all spiritual beings. Spiritual in this context doesn't mean the same as religious, although religion can nurture our spiritual nature. Embracing the Divine within is every bit as important to us in our search for the courage to be ourselves as are physical health, emotional stability, and mental clarity.

Spirituality brings us peace of mind and is, above all, an ever-expanding feeling of relationship with God as we understand Him/Her/It. Feeling connected to a source higher than ourselves gives us the desire to express love and be of service to others. It's popular these days to combine walking and spiritual awareness. I often sing hymns, pray, or practice gratitude as I walk. It lifts my spirit to commune with the Creatress as I move amid her beauty. For you, beautiful music, gazing at art, playing with children, or sitting quietly may create a feeling of spiritual balance and harmony within.

Most of us experience too little stillness, quiet, and solitude. Shakespeare said, "Sleep knits up the raveled sleeve of care." To this I would add, "Stillness knits up the raveled sleeve of soul" and "Stillness unravels the knitted brow of care." Stillness and solitude invite us to open to our authentic inner identity, which is, of course, our ultimate identity in this sphere of experience. In order for me to stay balanced, I must spend some quiet time every day with my special books and in prayer or meditation. What is your soul's food? When you discover what feeds you spiritually, make time to practice it often. Spirituality is like water; we need it to survive.

BALANCING OUR QUADRANTS

Much of our lives today are spent in our heads while our physical, emotional, and spiritual quadrants wither. All four areas need energizing. Slowly, gently make adjustments to your daily routine. Add a little exercise or a few quiet minutes alone. Be aware of your resistance to change and don't undermine your success by demanding the impossible. Make small alterations, build on your successes, and celebrate every change.

Filling up our life chalice before we fill others' takes courage because it seems to contradict the old dictums: "Think of others before you think of yourself" and "Live a life of service and sacrifice." In truth, we have little to give if our own chalice is depleted. When we fill our cups so that the overflow spills out to others, we'll be able to give more freely and willingly without an undercurrent of "Oh boy, do you owe me now!" Sensing when we're sharing from a sense of abundance, others are free to receive without guilt or obligation. We're giving to them and not expecting an equal return. We love and nourish best from overflow.

CLEANSING AND PROTECTION

A wonderful antidote to fear is learning ways to protect ourselves from absorbing other people's negative energy. The other ingredient in the fear-antidote is finding ways to cleanse our spirits when we do soak up and lug around that which isn't ours.

As you've undoubtedly noticed, the ability to pick up clues about how other people are feeling is both a blessing and a curse. The blessing is that we are able to use our intuition to know when someone around us needs a shoulder to cry or lean upon. The curse is that we can become emotional and psychic mega-vacs sweeping up gobs of emotional garbage that isn't ours. Other people's emotions that we have absorbed are often stored in the very cells of our own bodies.

While we are called to be of service to others, we are not meant to be pack mules designated to schlep everyone else's stuff. Usually our own stuff is weighty enough. As discussed earlier, carrying another's burden for/with them does nothing to lessen their load. We've merely leaped down into an emotional hole to join them. It's much better, when we are aware of another's pain, to compassionately—but with detachment—reach out a hand from the rim of the pit and help them to the top by caring about them, not carrying their stuff.

Sometimes we carry energy that isn't our own without even being aware of it. We may feel tired or depressed but not know why. Or we may experience a physical malaise but not be sick. In both cases, it's good to know how to free our bodies, minds, and spirits from uninvited energy.

There are many exercises, techniques, and prayers to help you cleanse and protect yourself. I will offer a few examples but also encourage you to tailor-make others to fit your individual beliefs and desires.

When I experience a feeling and can't put a finger on its origin, I say the following prayer: "Father/Mother God, if this is my feeling, I ask that I understand its cause and have the strength to work through it. If it is not my feeling, I ask that it be taken from me to its perfect, right place to be transformed and transmuted into the perfect, right energy." If I get the feeling that this isn't mine to deal with, I visualize angels or cherubs gathering up the energy and taking it away from me into the light of compassion.

A very simple way to cleanse any emotional grime from your body and soul is to stand under the shower and imagine the water moving through you as it washes over you. Invite the water to release from the very fabric of your being anything that isn't for your highest good. You don't even need to know what "it" is, but it does help to imagine what you don't want swirling down the drain.

Another great protection technique is to "put on the whole armor of God" as the Bible encourages us to do. My way of doing so probably has nothing to do with the biblical version, but it still works. If I'm giving a talk or doing anything that makes me feel vulnerable—a doctor's visit comes to mind—I imagine myself wrapped in a magic cloak that is invisible but powerful and protects me from all harm. One of my clients armored herself for a difficult custody hearing by imagining herself riding into the courtroom on a mighty bull (one that had a particular dislike for her former husband). She was amazed at how calm, grown-up, and unrufflable she felt atop her steed. Anytime fear popped up and her resolve waffled, she remembered her snorting bull and became an adult again. Imagination is a tremendously effective tool when we use it as our friend.

Take a moment now to allow your fertile imagination free reign. What might you do to protect yourself? How might you cleanse your body and soul from others' energy or your own negative energy? Play with the ideas that come up. Invite inspiration to flow through you and, most importantly, give yourself the gift of ways to cleanse and protect yourself from the toxic energy that we all encounter daily. Only then can you move beyond fear and become your beautiful and excellent spiritual self.

Finally, I want to share the Prayer of Protection with you, a prayer that has been extremely helpful to me and many others. During difficult times, I repeat it several times daily. It's very effective to recite it before you sleep and again as you wake. Saying it to my children as I tucked them in at night was a precious tradition to me as a mother, and now my daughter does the same with her sons.

Prayer of Protection

The light of God surrounds me (you).
The love of God enfolds me (you).
The power of God protects me (you).
The presence of God watches over me (you).
Wherever I am (you are), God Is.
And all is well.

—JAMES DILLET FREEMAN

CHAPTER TWELVE

THE POWER OF THOUGHT

As a matter of fact, we are always affirming something, be it for good or ill. We are always either saying, "I can" or "I cannot." What we need to do is to eliminate the negative and accentuate the positive. In doing this we shall gradually acquire the habit of affirmative thinking.

ERNEST HOLMES

The most profound agents of creation are invisible. The three that spring immediately to mind are God, biological conception, and thought. With enough technology, and no privacy whatsoever, we could probably monitor conception, but neither God nor thought can be made visible. We do, however, enjoy the benefits of God's creations each moment and also reap the fruits of our thoughts throughout our entire lives.

Wisdom teachers through the ages have taught about the awesome creative power of thought. The Buddha, for instance, said, "All that we are is the result of what we have thought." Ralph Waldo Emerson agreed and said, "What a man thinks of himself, that is which determines, or rather, indicates, his fate."

Mary Baker Eddy, founder of the Christian Science Church, said, "Stand porter at the door of thought. Admitting only such conclusions as you wish realized in bodily results, you will control yourself harmoniously." And the great sage, Anonymous (who was very often a woman!), states, "Sow a thought, and you reap an act; sow an act, and you reap a habit."

If you wonder about the power of thought, remember a dream that affected you deeply. Dreams are nocturnal thoughts that often cause reactions as intense as do actual occurrences. The other night I dreamed I was waiting at a train station for friends with whom I was going on a trip. Departure time loomed and no friends appeared. With each passing moment, I became more anxious. When I bolted awake, my heart was beating rapidly and I was awash in anxiety symptoms.

Usually we can sluff off the effects of dreams, but we cannot so easily avoid the consequences of habitual thought patterns. Thoughts act as powerful magnets drawing to us that which we fear or imagine. Luckily, thoughts are equal opportunity creators, and when we cultivate the habit of positive and affirmative thinking, they also draw wonderful people and experiences to us.

THINKING IS THE BIRTH OF FEELING

The last of the human freedoms is to choose one's attitude in any given set of circumstances.

VICTOR FRANKL

More than one thought track is generally active in our minds at the same time. Some are closer to the surface of consciousness than others, but we are constantly thinking and talking to ourselves. These internal conversations are called "self-talk."

Listen to what you're saying to yourself in the privacy of your own mind. If what you habitually tell yourself is optimistic, uplifting, and loving, you're certain to be a person who feels happy and energized. If the tone of your thoughts is self-recriminating, resistant, or pessimistic, you'll inevitably feel down and depressed. Thinking is the birth of feeling.

Negative, fearful self-talk undermines your self-esteem, creates painful feelings, and makes emotional strength difficult to attain. One of the quickest ways to become anxious is to let yourself worry about the future. I call this falling in the Future Hole. Future Hole self-talk statements often start out, "What if..."; "I couldn't handle..."; "I'm afraid that ...."

Our minds, if undisciplined, wander easily from the here and now into projections of the future. We need to plan for the future, but not worry. Planning creates security; worry creates anxiety. Planning is empowering; worrying accentuates helplessness.

Check your self-talk. How do you speak to yourself? Are you kind, encouraging, and upbeat? Would you talk similarly to a close friend? Are your thoughts contributing positively or negatively to your feelings? It isn't circumstance that creates our feelings; it's our thoughts about circumstances that give birth to our feelings.

Carrie had been unhappy in her marriage for a long time. She often said, "I wish Bill would just leave!" Finally Bill left and surprisingly Carrie fell apart. In her fear and grief about being alone, she forgot how unhappy they had been together and only concentrated on how awful she felt now that he was gone. She couldn't handle being abandoned, and she blamed herself totally. Her pain, some of which was natural, was exacerbated by her self-talk. The circumstance Carrie had desired was now made unbearable by what she was telling herself about it. She fell so far into a fear-filled Future Hole that she began drinking heavily to escape her feelings. This, of course, isolated her even more.

Carrie could have healed more quickly by becoming aware of her victimizing self-talk and choosing to replace it with supportive positive affirmations. For example, every time she found herself repeating the old, painful litanies, she could have said, "I am strong and able to handle all circumstances that come my way!"

Your feelings, and the thoughts that created them, are your own responsibility, nobody else's. If you want to change your feelings, take responsibility for changing your thoughts. Choosing to change your thoughts can release you from the victim role. When our thoughts and feelings are mainly positive, supportive, and life-affirming, self-esteem soars.

WHAT YOU THINK YOU ARE, YOU WILL BECOME

The unleased power of the atom has changed everything except our modes of thinking, and we thus drift toward unparalleled catastrophes.

ALBERT EINSTEIN

Imagine your mind as a garden. Which thoughts will you plant in it today? Negative, unhealthy, self-critical thoughts are like weeds. When you plant positive, healthy, constructive thoughts, you can expect a crop of beautiful flowers. Thus you alone determine whether your life looks like an overgrown weed patch or a well-tended, lushly beautiful flower garden.

If you've allowed your mind to drift along as it pleases for a long time (and most of us have), you'll need to train yourself gradually to become a healthy thinker. It helps to think of negative thoughts as unsettling music playing on the radio; you have the power to turn the dial to music you find enjoyable, soothing, and/or upbeat. You are just as able to change the dial on your negative self-talk. Without judgment, tune in to what you are thinking. If your thinking isn't leading your life toward healthy attitudes and positive feelings, you can choose to change the station.

Changing our thoughts is simple, which is not to say it's easy. No habit is easy to break, and unhealthy thinking is one of the most stubborn habits of all, one we may have built up over a lifetime. But have faith. What has been done, we can patiently undo. It will take practice and perseverance, but believe me, it is worth the challenge. Very simply, we choose to change our thinking, and then we formulate a plan of action. Here's an example from my life.

When I started to write this book, it became very clear to me that I was running full speed into a whole bevy of fears. In school I had always dreaded writing themes and essays, and the thought of writing a book terrified me. On the day of an important publishing meeting, I used hair spray instead of deodorant and lost my car in the parking lot where I'd parked for two years. I was completely spaced out, and no wonder. At the time, my dominant self-talk went like this: "What in the world do you think you're doing! You can't write! You got Cs in English (which wasn't true, but I felt as if I had). You must be crazy! You don't have anything to say."

Unhealthy self-talk swarmed in my head. So much so that my mind had become my enemy. I felt anxious and disoriented. Finally I remembered that I was in charge of what entered my mind and could change my thoughts. Tentatively I assured myself that I did have something to say. After all, I was a licensed therapist and had been successfully using the ideas I proposed to write about for years. Slowly I began to feel less anxious.

Why had I been sabotaging myself? I realized I was afraid that if I failed, I'd look stupid and have wasted a lot of time. If I succeeded, people might be jealous, and I still had residual painful memories from high school and family issues concerning jealousy. Fear of both failure and success were wrapped in the same package.

Unlike Katherine Hepburn who said, "I never realized until lately that women were supposed to be the inferior sex," I had realized we were supposed to be inferior. The book was pushing me out of my comfort zone, across limits beyond which I couldn't continue to function if I felt inferior. For me, to write was to risk.

I began to take the project more lightly. Someone once said, "Angels fly because they take themselves lightly." I had been taking writing so seriously I could hardly stagger along, let alone fly. I decided to SOAR: Stretch Out And Risk and enjoy the writing while I did it and have fun being an author if that dream came to fruition. Having chosen to think differently, I began to put into effect some well thought-out positive affirmations.

DEVELOPING INTO A HEALTHY THINKER

The select few who've mastered the art of meditation can empty their minds, but the rest of us can't stop thinking. Unfortunately much of what we think isn't conducive to strength, happiness, and self-esteem. Therefore, when we catch ourselves thinking negatively, we need to plan a script of thoughts to replace our unhealthy self-talk.

Admittedly I balked when first hearing the idea of creating a script for myself. Doing so seemed contrived and unnatural. Plus, I was convinced the whole idea was too simplistic to be effective. It wasn't until life pushed me over the edge and the slender thread by which I was hanging was being unraveled by my negative thoughts that I gave in and tried scripting. Because it worked—and still works—for me, I'm sharing it with you.

Avoid the common error of chastising yourself for negative thinking. If you catch yourself in the middle of some particularly negative self-talk and berate yourself, "There I go again! How terrible! No wonder I feel as I do! Why can't I stop this?", you'll only start a new line of negative, self-critical thoughts. Instead, give yourself a gold star for a good job of vigilant thought monitoring.

I watch my self-talk carefully. I was once working with a client who was suicidal. After the session I noticed I was feeling depressed and on the verge of tears. I tuned in to my self-talk. I'd been saying, "I should be able to save her. If she dies, I'll be responsible. I'm not up to the task of making her well." Ah, the Responsibility Sponge hard at work. No wonder I felt lousy.

I checked the reality of those debilitating thoughts and began to replace them with these: "She is a child of God, safe in the universe; I am a good therapist; I love myself and her." I pictured her well and happy and, as a result, began to feel better. Sad, still, but then it was a sad situation. But I changed the statements that were draining my self-esteem reserves and causing me pain and began to release my feelings of failure and fear, which, if continued, would have become obstacles to my helping her.

Affirmations are flower seeds that we plant in our subconscious. They have a powerful effect in helping us build a life that is happy, authentic, and free from fear. Conscious affirmations are an effective means of reprogramming negative self-talk, underlying assumptions, and hidden attitudes.

Probably the most important affirmation you can have is "I love myself." If you simply can't say that, as I couldn't when I started affirming, try "I am willing to love myself" or "I am willing to be willing to love myself." Whenever you become aware of unhealthy self-talk, replace it with one of the following affirmations or create your own affirmations to meet your particular needs:

POSITIVE SELF-TALK AFFIRMATIONS

1. I love myself.

2. I am a good friend to myself and others.

3. I am a worthwhile human being even though I make mistakes.

4. I know my limits and boundaries and stand up for them in a firm and loving manner.

5. I now have the time, energy, wisdom, and money to accomplish all that I desire.

6. I trust myself. I know what is good for me.

7. I am willing to be my ideal weight.

8. I am a valuable woman worthy of the love and respect of others.

9. I deserve satisfying and supportive relationships.

10. I am an excellent and creative worker.

11. I am wise, loving, light-hearted, and kind, a clear reflection of God.

12. I am God's (use any term that resonates with your heart) cherished daughter.

CREATING YOUR OWN AFFIRMATIONS

Because music etches ideas and words into our memory banks in ways that speaking doesn't, it is both fun and effective to sing our affirmations. A catchy little affirmation tune may run through your mind even if you're hardly aware of it. Such repetition encourages the subconscious to accept the statement as true.

To be effective, affirmations need to be in the present tense. Write your affirmations as if they were true now:

1. _____

2. _____

3. _____

4. _____

5. _____

We not only become what we think; we become what we picture and feel. While repeating your affirmations, picture the outcomes you would like from them as clearly and in as much detail as possible. If you're affirming that you're a worthwhile person, close your eyes and see or sense a picture of yourself being appreciated by others; or look in the mirror and tell yourself eye to eye how valuable and worthwhile you are. If you receive a note or card of appreciation, sit it on your desk or carry it with you and look at it often.

Don't expect quick results. You are reprogramming your subconscious mind, the most complex computer on earth. It will take time for your feelings to catch up with your new thoughts. But even if you don't feel the truth of the affirmation now, know that valuable work is being done on the subconscious level. The eventual benefits of changing thought patterns has been proven true over and over again by people who faithfully, persistently practice affirmations. These include world-class athletes and successful business people.

Think of the process of reprogramming your self-talk as being similar to training a puppy to the leash. At first, the puppy is confused and resistant. He digs in his little paws, puts his head down, and refuses to budge. Once he gets used to the idea, he runs ahead eagerly, enjoying the experience. Our feelings are comparable. As our inner language becomes self-loving and healthy, our feelings will surge ahead, eager to enjoy the journey.

As I did, you may hear a sneaky internal voice, sneering at your efforts and discounting any possibility of this dumb exercise working. It will tell you that you're bound to fail. It'll try to make you feel hopeless and helpless. It'll negate your right to be happy. It'll tell you that affirmations are too simple to be effective.

The following exercise is a good one for exorcising the inner Saboteur who stands over our shoulder and says, "Oh yeah!? Wanna bet!? Not on your life!" Neutralizing this voice is certainly worth it because nothing overruns our inner gardens as quickly or insidiously as negative thoughts and self-denigration.

Please take a blank sheet of paper and *print* carefully in the left column your affirmation; then in the right column quickly *write* any negative response from the Saboteur. Continue carefully printing the same affirmation in the left column and quickly dashing off all negative comments in the right column until you've ejected the Saboteur from the tape deck of your mind. Now you are ready to use your affirmation unhindered by internal deprecation and disbelief.

SELF-TALK SABOTEUR EXORCISM

affirmation (print carefully)	negative response (write quickly)
1. I love myself	You've got to be kidding.
2. I love myself.	Why? No one else does.
3. I love myself.	You don't deserve love.
4. I love myself.	You've done a lot of awful things.
5. I love myself.	You aren't spiritual enough.
6. I love myself.	Maybe a little, sometimes.
7. I love myself.	But you're twenty pounds overweight. You'll be lovable when you lose them.
8. I love myself.	You make so many mistakes...but you try hard.
9. I love myself.	I'm tired of writing this...
10. I love myself.	Okay, okay...
11. I love myself.	I do love myself... yes, I deserve love.

Use your affirmations faithfully. Choose how you will think. Picture yourself already experiencing the circumstances or attitudes you're affirming. Your reward will be a weed-free path toward being your best self.

Remember that nothing enters your mind without your consent. You are totally in charge of what you think. When worries plague you, put them on what my dad called his "2:00 a.m. Worrying List." Being a very sound sleeper, he rarely got to that list.

To help instill positive energy, read only materials that feed your soul and uplift your thoughts. Be with people who truly care for you and are positive, optimistic, and happy. Find ways to protect yourself from absorbing negative "vibes" projected at you. Don't subject yourself to negative TV and movie fare. While you may feel unaffected, your subconscious can carry the ideas (and fears) around for days, perhaps even years.

Planting thought-seeds of lack leaves you believing in and experiencing lack; planting thought-seeds of plenty helps assure that your life's harvest will be bountiful. It's up to you. You can believe that you can soar or you can allow limitations to clip your wings.

My son is a good example of the power of belief. His lifelong ambition was to be a professional athlete. During his senior year in high school, he severely injured his right knee and was told by a well-respected orthopedic surgeon that he'd never play sports again and that there was a good chance he'd walk with a limp for the rest of his life. We refused to believe in that limitation and searched until we found a knee specialist who gave us hope. Two years and three surgeries later, he completed his first triathlon race: a one-and-a-half-mile swim, a fifty-mile bike ride, and a thirteen-and-a-half-mile run. He chose to believe he could, and he did. You can too!

INTENTION AND INTUITION

Intention is the mother of self-invention. Setting your intention toward a goal, need, or attitude is akin to setting the autopilot on an airplane. We know where we want to go and we've set our course toward the desired destination. Consciously directed, intention becomes an invaluable ally in our quest for self-realization and the courage to express our authenticity.

Diana is a good example of the power of intention. She came to therapy because she was pregnant with her first child and wanted to be a good mom. "I'm not naturally maternal," she said. "I never wanted to babysit when I was a teenager and I don't have an ounce of patience with myself, let alone a kid." I admired both her candor and her desire to become what she felt she wasn't.

Diana's overall intention was to enjoy motherhood and to guide her child wisely and compassionately. Toward that end, she familiarized herself with babies and toddlers by seeking them out and offering to care for them. She read parenting books and created a wonderful list of affirmations that supported her goal. Probably her most important affirmation was "I trust myself completely and I know that I know."

Diana's daughter is now six and has a two-year-old brother. It's obvious that everyone in the family enjoys each other and that the children feel loved and secure. I was not surprised when Diana told me, "You know, being a mom isn't easy, but it's not as hard as I imagined. In fact, it's fun, and the kids are a kick." Having faced her fear, set her intention, planted many affirmative flower seeds, and then relaxed, she became the mother she wanted to be.

Intuition is sometimes described as "intellect without fear" and as "a state of knowing beyond logic and experience."

Thinker-friendly thoughts free our inner gardens from the weeds of negativity that choke out our intuition.

Intuition springs from the eternally astute core of our hearts and souls. It is a nonlinear certainty that "magically" makes itself known to us. Intuition can be seen as a spiritual compass, unerring and enduring in its guidance toward the expression of our higher selves and the realization of our highest good. However, intuition is a quiet voice usually perceived only when our hearts and minds are freed from the dulling cacophony of negative self-talk. Intuition is the voice of the Divine Feminine within. And, in essence, She is who we are.

CHAPTER THIRTEEN

YES, WE DO HAVE RIGHTS

I realized that if what we call human nature can
be changed, then absolutely anything is possible
and from that moment, my life changed.

SHIRLEY MACLAINE

Realities such as the "glass ceiling," sexual harassment, and the continuing poverty of older women and single mothers graphically let us know that, while we've come a long way, women still have a long way to go before attaining equal status, voice, respect, pay, and opportunity. Since changing inner attitudes, beliefs, and behaviors is the first and most essential step in changing the status quo, we must come to believe in our heart of hearts that we do indeed deserve to have equal rights and then courageously and constructively act on those beliefs. With time, effort, and commitment, we can bring about the needed changes.

I HAVE RIGHTS! OKAY?

For the most part, women have awakened to the realization that they do have emotional and practical rights and that it is essential and healthy for us to take care of ourselves and honor our own needs. We're beginning, tentatively and sometimes belligerently, to act on these realizations. But, it's not always easy. A Jules Feiffer cartoon I have illustrates the ambiguity with which many of us still struggle: A woman is standing with her arms wide and head thrown back jubilantly announcing, "I have motivation! I have self-esteem! I am taking control of my life!" In the next frame, her smile has faded and, in the next, she faces forward with a quizzical expression and says, "Okay?"

I don't know about you, but the dichotomy between what I *believe* about my rights and how I *feel* about asserting them is sometimes achingly similar to that cartoon.

A WOMAN'S BILL OF RIGHTS

To help myself, and the women with whom I work, overcome our fear of standing up for our rights, I compiled the following bill of rights. Some sentences come from long-forgotten sources, but the source I do remember well is my own life. In my journey toward being myself, I've struggled with each of these issues.

A Woman's Bill of Rights

1. I have the right to be treated with kindness and respect.

2. I have the right to be paid fairly for what I do.

3. I have the right to be listened to and taken seriously.

4. I have the right to take good care of myself.

5. I have the right to set my own priorities.

6. I have the right to say "No" without feeling guilty.

7. I have the right to seek my own spiritual truth.

8. I have the right to ask for the things I want and need.

9. I have the right to honor my creativity and pursue my dreams.

10. I have the right to laugh and have fun.

11. I have the right to have and express my feelings and opinions.

12. I have the right to love and be loved.

13. I have the right to be happy and have peace of mind.

14. I have the right and responsibility to be of service.

When you read the list, what is your response? If you can say, "Yes, I believe that—I have those rights in my life now," you are to be congratulated and emulated.

However, if some of the items make you shake your head and say, "Well, maybe, sometimes," or "You've got to be kidding! I could never feel that way! Even if I did, my family and friends would never honor it!" please read on.

The familiar adage "We teach people how to treat us" is very true. Before we can expect to be treated well, we must believe we deserve to be treated well. Before we can have our rights respected, we must believe that we have rights.

To help remind yourself that you do have rights, post a copy of the Woman's Bill of Rights, or a list of your own making, in a prominent place in your house and workplace, where it'll serve several purposes: it will help you remember what you're working toward, implant positive ideas in your subconscious mind, and make others aware of the goals you're striving for.

Kristy worked full-time, yet her husband and two sons expected her to assume full responsibility for the household as well. She went on strike—not just for a day or a week, but for three months. She shopped, cooked, and did laundry for herself but not for her family. Previously she'd been feeling victimized by her situation and unable to come up with a good solution; so she became increasingly resentful and angry. When she realized, "Yes, I have rights, too!" and went on strike, the angry feelings disappeared.

Kristy was willing to risk her family's displeasure and, at first, she did take a lot of flak. Her husband and sons teased and humored her, thinking she was kidding; by the second week they were furious because they could see how much they'd been demanding and knew they were going to have to change. Her strike succeeded; Kristy now has three willing coworkers.

RISK: TAKING RESPONSIBILITY AND MAKING CREATIVE CHOICES

Growth requires the ability and willingness to risk, of courting the unexpected. Risking is scary, but without risk we are unable to throw off the chains of emotional dependence and second-class citizenship. In her book *What's Holding You Back?*, Dr. Linda Austin addresses the issues that keep women from shattering actual and self-imposed glass ceilings. Concerning risk taking, she says,

Women can learn to take risks, intelligent risks. There needs to be a process of gradually increasing the capacity for risks. The place to start is in risky thoughts. What you allow yourself to think about and whether you allow yourself to challenge old ideas that you've had, or old myths, old assumptions, that you've had about your life. The second level of risk taking is with your speech. Do you allow yourself to speak up, do you speak the truth as you see it, do you talk in meetings? And the third level is in your behavior and the things that you usually do.

Each risky thought we entertain, each time we speak up and out no matter the consequences, and each time we act in a new and daring way, we not only increase our inner and outer freedom but also widen the path to freedom for others to follow. With gratitude, I think of the women before us who were brave enough to demand the vote and insist on the right to keep property when they married. They forged a trail in consciousness for the rest of us, just as surely as the pioneers broke trails to the West.

Women's new path of consciousness has a few visible, historic landmarks, but for the most part it is an invisible trail, felt more than seen. It has been built and paved by the courage, hopes, tears, and fears of the women who've gone before us. Every risk we take makes it easier for others to summon the courage to risk being themselves. By creating new patterns for our own actions, we create patterns that respect the rights of all, both women and men.

Also, each time we risk saying or doing what feels right to us, we are taking responsibility for our own lives. While your life is no one's responsibility but your own, there are also things in your life over which you have no control and for which you aren't responsible. However, we are responsible for how we respond to any circumstance. And our response alone determines whether circumstances become resolved positively or linger indefinitely draining our energy and lust for life.

When we become response-able—that is, when we learn to choose our responses freely and consciously—we are free to build a life of continuing growth and increasing happiness.

For those circumstances in life over which we have no control, such as emotional hurts received in early childhood, we can learn to take responsibility for our need to grieve, and make creative choices regarding how we will do so.

Victoria, about whom I spoke earlier, was the victim of violent sexual abuse from infancy until eighteen years of age. She was not responsible for that early pain, but she is responsible for her response and rehabilitation. Victoria must grieve; at this point her pain is so great that she simply has no choice. But she is free to choose how she will grieve. Although her struggle is a mighty one, she is risking by experiencing her pain, taking responsibility for her healing, and making creative choices. She is also reaching out to others with similar pain, which is a sure sign of healing.

Even if we have not endured trauma as atrocious as Victoria has, all of us bear scars that affect how we lead our lives. Taking responsibility for healing those old wounds is taking responsibility for the way our lives can be from now on. Ask yourself: If I took responsibility for this situation in my life and my response to it, how could I alter, heal, avoid, solve, stop, work with, or change it?

If you started counting on yourself for solutions, where would you start? What's the first, tiny baby step that you can take? Don't worry about the overall dimensions of the process; just take that one small step. If you need moral support, talk with a friend or professional counselor. But, please, for your own well-being, risk taking one small step at a time toward needed change.

If we persist in thinking that "they" need to change before we can be happy, we'll never get anywhere. Whether "they" are our family, mate, friend, the economy, the weather, a circumstance, or unloving parents, if we rely on them to change our lives for us—good luck. We're stuck! When we realize that we're responsible—not blameworthy, but responsible—for our own lives and happiness, we'll begin building the inner power to change and make creative choices. If, for example, your husband is an alcoholic, you have several choices. You can blame the situation and be a victim, go to Al-Anon, or investigate other practical steps toward creating a living environment in which you can thrive.

Feeling dull and lifeless? What dragon inside you is keeping your sparkle from shining through to the surface? Choose to take responsibility for healing yourself. Stretch out and risk exploring your life patterns to find out what's going on. Find ways to infuse yourself with enthusiasm. You cannot feel bored, dull, or lifeless, and enthusiastic at the same time.

Every change risks a crisis. As we start changing our responses to circumstances, we'll undoubtedly upset some of the people in our lives. People resist change, and they are familiar with us as we are. The Chinese character for "crisis" is a combination of the characters for "danger" and "opportunity." Risking change creates danger to the limiting status quo, but opens up new and freeing opportunities for ourselves, our families, and our friends. Risk may be frightening, but it brings tremendous rewards. We all need to go for it!

As Shirley Briggs says, "Let's dare to be ourselves, for we do that better than anyone else can." It's your life; don't waste it. You can chart a path toward a happier life by accepting the fact that you are responsible for changing what needs to be changed and for choosing a creative course of action that will enhance self-esteem, increase emotional strength, and instill the courage to be yourself.

SPEAKING OUT WITHOUT BLOWING UP

With good reason many of us seem to suffer from conflict-aphobia. We may bear emotional scars as the result of poorly handled conflicts or being chastised for attempting confrontation of any sort. What a bind that puts us in because the more we can speak our truth and solve conflicts amiably and equitably, the better off everyone is. Therefore it is a good thing for us to learn to communicate constructively and, by example and expectation, help those around us do likewise.

The following poem by William Blake points out one of the major reasons it's important for us to express ourselves:

> I was angry with my friend;
> I told my wrath, my wrath did end.
> I was angry with my foe;
> I told it not, my wrath did grow.

As we choose risky new behaviors that may threaten others, it's especially vital that we know how to speak up for ourselves. There are two ways to tell our wrath: the constructive and destructive. We've all seen (and probably used) the destructive methods: hiding feelings or blowing our tops and spewing out raw emotions in people's faces. Destructive communication causes our wrath and the wrath of others to *grow,* rather than to *go.*

How can we speak out without blowing up or causing others to blow up? Actually we don't have control over how others respond, but we can learn to communicate in ways that lessen the possibility of defensive responses.

First, convince yourself that you have the right to speak out. If you need to refresh your memory, refer to the Bill of Rights on page 176. You may also want to search your consciousness for seed sentences that are preventing others from hearing and respecting your words. One of mine used to be, "If you don't have anything nice to say, don't say anything at all." I surrounded myself with friends who'd been trained as I had and were, therefore, fellow conflictaphobes, afraid of confrontation and honest communication. If I voiced my feelings and was told that what I had to say wasn't "nice," I believed it. So for years I stuffed my feelings back inside even when I needed to share them, fearing I'd be rejected, labeled a bitch, or disturb the peace of any relationship.

Once we believe we have a right to voice our feelings and opinions, we need to learn how to speak out constructively. Speaking out in order to make others see an issue our way, to convince them, or to prove them wrong, is acting destructively. We need to learn to speak out with the goal of understanding each other: speaking without blame, and listening without judgment.

Blowing up constructively is like taking out the garbage. Our minds create emotional garbage that in turn creates harmful toxins in our bodies. If we don't blow up, and blow off those toxins, chances are we'll "blow in" and create suppression-related maladies such as depression, heart disease, and even cancer. Instead of blowing up, lots of women blow *out,* i.e., get fat. I can always tell when I'm holding something back because I put on weight.

There's an art to blowing up constructively. When our inner dragons have built up a good head of steam, we do need to blow it out, but it's essential to aim it away from people and breakable objects. Little children know innately how to blow up. They fling themselves on the floor and pound and kick. Very rarely do they hurt themselves.

Wise parents and teachers call time-outs to allow kids to express themselves. The child can go off by herself and express to her heart's content. How about giving yourself time-outs? Take the force of your anger and frustration away from people, and let 'er rip. Only then speak out.

If you really go for it while you blow up, you'll feel tired but cleansed. I believe Robert Frost's statement, "The best way out is always through," is true of our emotions.

After taking a time-out to go through emotions and thereby release excess energy, we can more easily talk and listen constructively, with the help of a few simple communication tools.

TOOLS FOR CONSTRUCTIVE COMMUNICATION

A. Prepare for Communication by:

1. Blowing up privately.

2. Clarifying what you're feeling and what you want to say.

    a. Make notes to yourself. A client of mine takes an emotional memo to herself, labeled "Memo to Me: I'm angry about (___)." She writes down her feelings and puts them in the "IN" basket to be worked out at a more convenient time. It's important that you can trust yourself to always come back to those "IN" files, if only to see if your feelings are now clear. If you don't check back, it's probably a sign you wish to suppress those feelings.

b. Organize what you want to communicate.

c. Rehearse what you intend to say.

Remember, communication isn't guerrilla warfare. The reason for speaking out is to create greater understanding, love, and intimacy.

B. Timing

I can't stress enough how important timing is to good communication. It's essential. Many people ruin any chance for constructive communication by choosing the wrong time to speak. Those four little words, "We have to talk," strike terror in the hearts of people who are afraid of confrontation. If we add "now!", we're setting ourselves up to be met defensively. It's only fair that both parties agree on the time to talk.

Over the years my husband and I have evolved a system that works for us. If I want to talk, I tell him I need to talk sometime within the next twenty-four hours. I tell him the subject—in one or two sentences, maximum. Then I let him know just how big a deal it is for me by using the "on a scale from 1 to 10" measurement. Since he can choose the time, which needs to be mutually agreeable, he has a sense of being empowered in the process. If I were to jump on him and demand that we talk "right now," he'd feel attacked and defensive. I know, because I've done it and it didn't work.

When he chooses the time, he can gather his thoughts on the subject; he can prepare. Some people find it helps to make regular appointments to discuss anything that has come up, or have a "clear the air" dinner once a week, or perhaps schedule ten or twenty minutes each evening specifically to talk. Whatever works for you is fine.

C. Communicating

1. *Restate your goal.* Before you start talking, take a few deep breaths, hold hands, and each state your goal for the discussion. What do you hope to gain? Learn? Understand? If you stray from the subject, remind each other.

2. *Share how you feel.* As you begin the discussion, what are your fears and physical symptoms? Instead of protecting yourself behind masks of attack, indifference, or bravado, show your vulnerabilities. When I need to talk about something uncomfortable, my body gets very anxious. So I might say, "This is really hard for me. My heart is racing and my stomach is upset. I'm perspiring and my tongue feels as big and dry as a throw rug."

3. *Check your reality.* Sometimes what we perceive from the other person isn't what was intended. Before you react, check out your assumptions by saying something like, "I need a reality check," "I feel shut out," or "Are you angry with me?" If the answer is yes, you can choose to pursue it now or later. If the answer is no, accept it. If your feeling persists, check it out again.

4. *Use "I Messages."* "I Messages" are excellent ways to help eliminate defensiveness. The formula is: "When you do/say (_____), I feel (_____)." The idea is to express real feelings, not judgments or accusations. Use one or two words at most to describe a real

feeling. Examples of feelings: hurt, confused, tired, angry, joyful, uncomfortable, abandoned, or excited. Feelings describe what's happening to you, rather than a judgment about whatever the other person is doing. Here's an example of a clear "I Message": "When you talk to me in that tone of voice, I feel hurt and angry."

By contrast, "You Messages" point fingers, make judgments, criticize personally, and interpret. The "I Message" above could have been sent as a "You Message": "When you talk to me in that tone of voice, you're doing it just to hurt me!" or "You make me feel awful. You hurt me!" The silent tag line at the end of a "You Message" is "You bastard, you!" "I Messages" inform. "You Messages" attack.

Examples:

"YOU MESSAGES"	"I MESSAGES"
You are disgusting and irresponsible when you drink.	When you drink, I feel scared and disgusted.
You are rude and irresponsible not to call when you are going to be late.	I worry and feel like an abandoned kid when you don't call if you are going to be late.
You are an insensitive bully to tease me when you know it hurts me.	When you tease me, I feel helpless and angry.

D. Nonverbal Communication

One of my clients was in the hospital after the birth of her son. Her mother-in-law visited her and said, "I saw you had a lot of flowers yesterday, so I brought you something today." She handed her a small, unwrapped cactus still boasting its seventy-nine-cent Safeway price tag. What a blatant, nonverbal put-down.

Actions speak louder than words. When our nonverbal messages are out of sync with our words, everyone gets confused. We've all had the experience of being in the presence of someone who was acting so cold that your nose hairs froze, yet when asked what was wrong they said (frostily), "Nothing!" That's a mixed (or double) message: words conflicting with action and attitude.

E. Listening

Listening is probably the most important part of any communication. Listening leads to understanding and creates a bridge to intimacy. Here are some suggestions to foster good listening.

1. *Allow pauses.* Before you formulate a response, be sure you've taken time to really hear what the other person has said. Resist the tendency to race ahead of his or her thoughts, stacking up retort ammunition.

    Silent pauses are an essential feature of real communication. If you keep trying to break in while the other person is talking, you are not listening. People can't communicate unless you affirm their worth by allowing them to really be heard. Understanding requires true hearing. Relationships thrive on understanding. If you want to have successful relationships, listen. Really listen.

Interestingly, "listen" and "silent" contain the same letters.

2. *Reflect back.* Restate what you believe your communication partner has just said. If you've ever played the parlor game Gossip (also called Telephone), where a message gets passed around a circle by one person whispering it to the next, you know that messages easily get distorted by being misheard. Verify that you've heard correctly. Make sure you're both talking about the same issue or feeling. Say something like, "When you said 'I guess it would be okay' for me to go to the movies with Nancy on Friday night, were you asking me not to go?"

Don't assume you know what's meant. You know what they say about *assume:* it makes an "ass" out of "u" and "me."

Reflect. Explore. Make sure you understand. To respectfully and lovingly listen takes patience and desire. The rewards are well worth it.

HONORING WHAT WE WANT AND NEED

Why do women leave home to take their services into the marketplace? Money? For sure. But maybe they felt the need to materialize. You had to have been there to know what it was like to be invisible. To move and not be seen, to talk and not be heard. To have family return to the house every evening and say, "Anyone home?"

ERMA BOMBECK

Have you ever felt invisible? Who alone of all the people you know has the power to make you visible? You! And you'll never become visible unless you honor your wants and needs.

What is it you want and need? Affection? Approval? Love? Hugs? To succeed? To be heard? To have help around the house? Do you ask for help filling those wants and needs, or do you hope people will psychically "know" about them without your asking? That's not fair. Expecting people to read your mind hardly ever gets you what you desire.

Simone, a teacher, was going through her second divorce and feeling bereft and worthless. Finally she worked up the courage to ask for what she needed: lots of hugs and acknowledgment that she was okay, even though twice divorced. She made a badge, which she wore at school. It said: "I need eight hugs a day!" Her willingness to ask for what she wanted sparked a wonderful revolution at her school. Soon people were not only hugging her but hugging others as well. A climate of closeness developed among the staff that hadn't existed in the pre-hug days.

Other people can never give us all that we want and need, so we must also learn to fill many of our wants and needs ourselves.

Pat is newly single and also needs love and hugs. Her underlying need for affection had its origins in a nonsupportive relationship with her mother. Her separation from her husband only exacerbated her feelings of abandonment. Pat's inner little girl is crying for loving acceptance.

I keep a large, soft doll in my office, and when I gave it to Pat to hold, she poured out to it all the love that her inner child craved. I encouraged her to buy herself a doll or teddy bear. Silly as it sounds, it helps. Hugging, holding, talking to an accepting cuddly toy (or a real, live pet) encourages us to develop gentle, healing attitudes toward our inner child. You might try hugging several bears or dolls in the store until you find one that feels just right to you.

Pat's case is a good example of how external objects can help us explore our inner wants and needs, and honor them. We have a right to know our needs and fulfill them. We can explore ways to ask for what we need, and learn to fill our own needs ourselves.

As we gain confidence in our rights and learn to honor our wants and needs, we'll open doors to inner wholeness and health. We'll move beyond dependence and find the courage to be ourselves. In the process, we'll be better able to discover and honor our own excellence and encourage others to do the same.

CHAPTER FOURTEEN

BEING A LOVING AND ACCEPTING FRIEND TO YOURSELF

A true friend
        brings out the best in us

While knowing the worst.

Even though privileged
        to our darkest fears and frailties,

A true friend believes in
        our goodness and worth;

Our inherent ability to
        survive and thrive.

A true friend
        acts as a confessional
                in which we transform guilt
        and a kiln in which we
                fire our strength.

True friends are
        essential.

I 've heard it said that love is the "Open Sesame" of life. And, of course, the first heart to open is our own. If you have yet to master the magic key to self-love, what do you need to do, feel, or think in order to love yourself more fully? For me, shoring up my belief in my prevailing goodness is a great help. From the neck up, I know that I never do anything purposely hurtful, but during descents into the underbelly of my psyche, I sometimes lose my knowing about my innate goodness.

During one such descent recently, I was trying to regain my equilibrium by meditating on a picture of a labyrinth that I had finger-walked around at church that morning. As I imagined myself walking the curves and U-turns of the labyrinth, the meditation took on a life of its own and I was propelled along, no longer in control of the experience. (Believe me, this is unusual for me.) Arriving at the center of the labyrinth, I was met by two divine beings who "showed" me the depth of my own goodness. It was a visceral, through-to-the-bone experience. Vastly moving and very tearful.

I wish I could say that I'll never doubt myself or my goodness again, but that wouldn't be a truthful statement because I know the depth of the patterns with which I am contending. I do, however, carry within the very fabric of my soul a powerful and healing memory of the feeling the experience elicited in me. My intention is to instill its truth in the core of my being by being a bit more self-accepting and self-loving daily. Although not a cure, the meditation has definitely provided me with a valuable touchstone to which I can return when needed.

What "Open Sesame" do you need to adopt in order to open your heart and become a true friend to yourself? Take a moment to think about how you treat your friends. Do you extend the same kindness, compassion, and consideration to yourself? Many of us hold a deep-rooted belief that we don't deserve to be loved. "They" might deserve friendship, but for some unfathomable reason, we don't. This is a false belief. We are worthy of love. We do deserve our own support and friendship as well as the love, acceptance, and friendship of others.

FRIENDSHIP IS ESSENTIAL

To most women, friendship is not a luxury; it is an essential part of their being. Because connection with ourselves and others is our most valued lifeline, it is much more difficult to become our authentic selves if we are attempting to do so in a vacuum, without the intimacy of friendship as ballast. Having the support and unconditional love of a few true friends, ones who can mirror our wonderfulness to us in the midst of any circumstance, gives us the boost we need to tackle almost anything. Of course, we can survive without friendship, but can we thrive? I think not.

Unfortunately there are times when we are so totally disconnected from ourselves that we become our own worst enemy. No matter how many legions of external friends we may have, survival seems the best we can do. In those periods of internal crisis, who comforts, guides, and nurtures us back to balance and harmony? More often than not, our friends do. Friendship is the finest balm for bruises of the spirit—and darn good company during bouts of silliness and fits of giggles as well.

Joyce decided that her role with her adult children was to be their most supportive cheerleader and only give advice when specifically asked. "How great! What a wonderful idea! I know you can do it!" she tells them often. In talking about her decision, we decided that cheerleading was something we could all use more of and so agreed to be cheerleaders for each other. We even chose the color of pom-poms we preferred.

During the inevitable ups and downs of family life and the work/play of revising this book, Joyce has been a wonderful cheerleader for me. Hearing her cheer, "You go, girl!", "What a wise and good thing to have said!," and sometimes a simple, "Rah, rah, rah..." lightens the energy, makes me laugh, and helps me believe in myself. With her as my role model, it's easier for me to remember to be my own enthusiastic cheerleader.

Remembering is one of the main "Open Sesame" keys to self-love and friendship, isn't it? When I remember that cheerleading is an option, I'm more likely to do it for myself and others when the opportunity or need arises. When we remember that it is essential we become our own loving and accepting friends, that mind-set slowly begins to take root within us and eventually becomes an integral part of who we are and how we act.

One excellent tool to help us remember our unique gifts is the commitment to give ourselves credit.

GIVING YOURSELF CREDIT

In his book, *Kinship with All Life*, J. Allen Boone states, "The most effective way to achieve right relations with any living thing is to look first for the best in it, and then help that best into the fullest expression." What about right relations with self? Do you find it easy to see and credit the best in others but have trouble believing in and crediting the best in yourself?

If so, to help rectify that incongruity, let's imagine that our lives are like a bank account in which we make deposits and withdrawals. How often do you credit the account of your body, emotions, mind, and spirit? We all have a life account, which we frequently deplete or allow others to withdraw from too freely. In order to have a comfortable "balance" and not "see red"—experience frustration and anger—we need to credit liberally and debit wisely in all areas of our lives.

EMOTIONAL BANK ACCOUNT

Debits

Unhealed wounds	Perfectionism
Self-condemnation	Isolation
Overwork	Unreasonable expectations
Judgment	Resistance

A negative life-balance, caused by too many debits, leads to emotional overdrafts such as:

Low self-esteem	Depression
Overweight	Exhaustion
Emotional vulnerability	Loss of self
Unhappiness	Illness

Credits

Setting limits	Healing old wounds
Self-acceptance	Friends
Exercise	Solitude
Listening to yourself	Love

Credits, which create a positive life-balance, lead to emotional surpluses such as:

High self-esteem	Authenticity
Energy	Joy
Self-confidence	Healing
Courage	Fulfilling relationships

Debit and Credit Examples

DEBIT	CREDIT
"How stupid can you be?"	"Everyone makes mistakes; I'll do better next time."
"Yes" (when you mean "no")	"No, I'm sorry. I am not able to do (____)."
Feeling guilty	Apologizing for real slights and mistakes
"Everything's just fine." (false smile)	Being truthful about your feelings
"No, I don't need a thing."	"What I could use is a good hug!"
"I never do as well as who's-it."	"Great! I did that better than before."
"You Messages" (saying things you'll regret	"I Messages" (not gunnysacking)
Overscheduling and rushing	Realistic goals and schedules
No time for yourself	Relaxing: enjoying your own company
Oversitting; lots of TV	Doing enjoyable exercise
Concentrating on your failures	Celebrating your successes

You alone are in charge of your emotional bank account. Other people should be allowed to withdraw or credit your account only if and when you give them permission.

Be liberal with deposits and discerning about withdrawals. Never write a blank check.

GOLD STAR LISTS

When I was a novice at being kind and friendly toward myself, I faithfully made gold star lists. At day's end, I listed at least six things I'd said, done, or felt during the day that deserved a gold star. I still do it whenever I'm having a hard time being gentle with myself. This little appreciation exercise works well for both myself and clients because it teaches us to focus on our positive qualities, to give ourselves credit.

Make a list of your own. Rate your actions relatively. For example, on a day when you're feeling depressed or are ill, give yourself a gold star for getting out of bed and brushing your teeth. Be a little creative and outrageous. Your list doesn't have to be all goody-two-shoes items. I recently rewarded myself with three gold stars for having a rip-roaring, constructive temper tantrum. I beat a couch with a stuffed sock, screamed, and had a good cry. One star was for giving myself permission to be angry, one for not directing my rage at anybody, and the other for not feeling guilty afterward.

Your list will be unique to you depending on your emotional strength and self-esteem that day. It might run the gamut from "I didn't call myself stupid all day" to "It was gutsy and fun to run that marathon. I'm proud of myself!" Buy yourself a packet of gold stars and become your own cheerleader. It's fun and an A+ way to turn your powerful mind into a good friend.

When my husband and I were talking about taking a day trip as a reward for finishing the first draft of this revision, he said, "There's no such thing as too many rewards!" He meant there is no such thing as too many *self*-generated rewards, and I couldn't agree more. We can benefit greatly from granting ourselves deserved rewards, bonuses that say, "Well done!"

Good friends support and gift each other with generous dollops of appreciation and recognition. It's only appropriate that we do the same for ourselves.

Becoming aware of our strengths and attributes is one of the best rewards we can give ourselves on the road toward being our authentic selves. And sometimes we simply need to get in the habit of giving ourselves credit in order to realize that our true potential for love, creativity, compassion, self-realization, and service is boundless and sorely needed by ourselves, our families, our friends, our entire world.

WWW.WEB4WOMEN

I have a fantasy that we could use our burgeoning technology as a friendly support system for women. What if someone created Web sites such as whoami?.com or losingmyself.argh that sweetly and nonjudgmentally encouraged harried women to take a break, breathe, and ask: "Is what I'm doing right now necessary? Am I freely choosing to do it? If not, why am I doing it? Is fear my motivator? Who within me is feeling hurt, scared, or pressured?"

After gently being guided to our perfect, right answers, we would automatically be linked to gimmegoldstars.net where a kindly voice—a cyber Mr./Ms. Rogers—would assure us that we are wonderful just the way we are. That's credit we'd all enjoy.

THE GIFT OF FORGIVENESS

Forgiveness is a precious gift we give ourselves. The ability to forgive both ourselves and others is another of the magic keys that can open Freedom's Gate.

One of the most basic reasons for practicing forgiveness is that old stuff, old pains and wounds—no matter how far in the past—still feel fresh and create the same responses in the body, mind, and spirit when we hold on to the feeling. A former inmate of a Nazi concentration camp was visiting a friend who had shared the ordeal with her.

"Have you forgiven the Nazis?" she asked her friend.

"Yes."

"Well, I haven't. I'm still consumed with anger and hatred," the visitor said.

Her friend gently replied, "Then they still have you in prison."

One woman had been able to let go of the past and walk in freedom's light. Sadly the other was still chained to the darkness of past torment and, consequently, also bound to her tormentors.

FORGIVING OTHERS

Most of us do not need to forgive such severe atrocities, but all of us have been wounded and disappointed during the course of our lives. Forgiveness originally meant to "return good treatment for ill usage," which reminds me of a beautiful quote: "Forgiveness is the fragrance the violet sheds on the hand that has crushed it." Each of us is susceptible to human failings. We've all pointed the finger of blame and have trotted out Ms. Righteous Indignation to bludgeon ourselves and our loved ones. We will, or have, crushed the delicate violet of another's feelings and have had ours crushed as well. Forgiveness is the only way to free ourselves from the regrets of the past and move on with our lives.

Lack of forgiveness gives others power over us. Withholding forgiveness simply allows another person to have control over our well-being. An aphorism that underscores this reality says, "Holding a grudge is like taking poison and hoping it hurts the other person." Hanging on to negative, pessimistic, or painful feelings puts a crimp in the flow of our life-force and personal power, damming them from coursing through us as effectively as we can stop water from flowing through a hose by stepping on it. The Buddha sums this up nicely by saying, "When one person hates another, it is the hater who falls ill—physically, emotionally, and spiritually. When he loves, it is he who becomes whole. Hatred kills, love heals." As the Buddha knew, just for the health of it we need to gift ourselves with forgiveness. Forgiveness frees us from the influence of others and reconnects us to our own sense of empowerment.

There is a difference between healthy and unhealthy forgiveness. For example, Robert Enright, Ph.D., an education psychologist at the University of Wisconsin-Madison, stressed that true forgiveness is not:

- Forgetting. If the wound is deep enough, we may always retain a memory of it.

- Excusing or condoning. We need not deny, minimize, or justify a wrong.

- Reconciling. We can forgive a person and still choose not to be in relationship with him or her.

- Weakness. It shows strength and wisdom to free ourselves from the emotional chains of non-forgiveness.

The best ways I've found for starting the forgiving process are first to solidify your intention. What do you desire for your own well-being? You may affirm something along the lines of "I want to forgive. I will forgive. I do forgive." Next, remind yourself what forgiving is not. You don't need to forget, condone, or become chummy. Neither are you weak for perfecting the art of forgiveness. You are, instead, courageously freeing yourself to move on.

As we commit to letting go of past hurts and present pain, affirmations and prayer are powerful aides. Formulate affirmations that state your intention to forgive, and use them whenever your mind picks at the scab of your wound. For instance, when my first husband fell in love with my best friend, I wanted to forgive for my own good. But the best I could do early on was affirm: "I am willing to be willing to forgive him, her, and myself." Gradually I progressed to "I forgive us all." Eventually the sweet feeling of forgiveness flowed into my heart and I was free. Over the years forgiveness has turned to gratitude. What felt like a horrendous betrayal actually opened the way to a much happier life.

Along with all our personal efforts toward forgiveness, it's always helpful to surrender the feelings and struggles to God. I might say, "I'm hurt, Mother/Father God. This wound is so unfair that I need your help to forgive. Please send your love, compassion, and forgiveness through me to _____." Then I might pray, "With your help, I forgive _____."

As much as possible, give up your expectations about how long the forgiving process should take and be consciously accepting and gentle with yourself as you release and recover. As we move through the forgiving process, it's especially important to nurture your inner self.

FORGIVING YOURSELF

Not being able to forgive ourselves is virtually an insurmountable barrier to becoming our own good friends. If we evaluate our performance in life by immediately recalling acts of kindness, courage, or thoughtfulness that we "should" have done but didn't, or dredging up the "bad" things we did do or imagined we did, naturally forgiveness is difficult.

Of course we do things that require forgiveness. The beauty of such cliches as "To err is human, to forgive, divine" is that, without the immutable truth embedded in their core, they would never have become cliches. We do err.

Elisabeth Kübler-Ross, M.D, a psychiatrist and specialist in the field of death and dying, calls Earth "the hospital planet." We are all here to recover and heal. Each of us carries internal wounds. We all grope for what is right. And we can courageously accept responsibility for our failures and foibles, make amends if possible, and forgive ourselves as we would a treasured friend. Forgiveness creates an atmosphere in which we can best heal.

An interesting study, written several years ago in *Psychology Today*, reported that several sports psychologists had compared world-class athletes with athletes who were never quite able to fulfill their potential. The difference, they discovered, was that the world-class athletes were able to forgive their mistakes immediately and carry on, while second-class athletes browbeat themselves whenever they made a mistake. This research underscores the idea that the ability to forgive ourselves is rewarded with success, while feeling guilty and beating up on ourselves is penalized with failure.

Negativity never heals negativity. My spiritual mother, Annabelle, says, "You can't get rid of the darkness by beating at it with a stick. You must turn on the light." In many cases, the light is that of self-forgiveness.

To facilitate forgiving yourself, it often helps to think frequently of your inner child. Treat her with gentleness, forgiveness, and tolerance. Whenever I fail, do something foolish, or feel a need to be forgiven, I very deliberately think of myself as "Susie Q." Reverting to my childhood name helps me remember my inner little girl and soften my attitude toward myself.

I once received a very helpful button from a minister. It said PBPWM GIFWMY, which decoded means Please Be Patient With Me: God Isn't Finished With Me Yet!

What affirmations come to mind that would help you be patient with and forgiving of yourself? One of my early favorites to neutralize old perfectionism patterns was "I made a mistake, so sue me!" Although not a true affirmation, this sassy statement was good for me because I tended to take my mistakes much too seriously, especially when I was a young mom.

Appropriate forgiving affirmations are similar to the following: "I forgive myself for _____. I love and accept myself even though I'm not perfect. I forgive myself because I know I did the best I could at the time. I am willing to forgive myself. I am a caring woman, worthy of forgiveness."

You will know the affirmative statements that best fit your situation. And please remember that you may need to say or sing them repeatedly in order to replace habitual, devaluing, and non-forgiving inner scripts. That's okay.

We are always talking to ourselves. In our minds, we create stories about ourselves based on our current experiences as well as experiences from the past. Too often we cast ourselves in the role of "bad girl"—that schmucky little kid who never quite measured up, the one who needed to be perfect in order to deserve to live, the victim, the phony, the antagonist.

The people around us when we were young helped us create these stories. Many families have a "bad kid" and a "good kid," a "smart kid" and a "dumb kid," an "everybody's favorite" and a "black sheep," a "responsible kid" and a "baby."

Unconsciously, we carry these labels into adulthood where they become our history and often our legacy. But we now have the awareness and power to re-choose and re-create our stories. We can begin to tell stories about ourselves that are positive, encouraging, tolerant, forgiving, gentle, hopeful, and loving.

Compare:

> "Good grief, you forgot to mail that report (get a sitter, whatever)! Can't you remember anything? You're probably getting senile! You have been really stupid lately. You are either sick, or you're really losing it! You should at least be able to remember (____)!"

With:

> "Susie Q, you are really forgetful lately. What's going on? Are you running on overload, feeling sick, or burning out? What do you want and/or need from me to make it better?"

The first story is very destructive. It lays the groundwork for fears of illness and failure, and definitely is not conducive to forgiveness. The second story is constructive and self-loving.

The subconscious is like wet clay: it retains the imprint of whatever we press into it and then it faithfully reproduces that imprint in our lives. For instance, if we tell ourselves stories that imply we don't deserve to be loved, to succeed, or to lose weight, our subconscious will keep us unloved, failing, and chubby.

Women in workshops that I've done have found the following exercise to be both enjoyable and illuminating. Try it and see what looking through the eyes of love does to your history. Review your past and rewrite it as if you were a dear friend who sees the best in you and loves and accepts you unconditionally. Rewrite your personal history as an internal cheerleader might if she were the author.

To give yourself the priceless gift of forgiveness:

- Accept responsibility for your actions and attitudes and right any wrongs you can.

- Apologize if warranted. If a sincere apology is not accepted, groveling is not required.

- Create affirmations that out-sing the inner critic and highlight your true friendship with yourself.

- Tell yourself optimistic, realistic, and friendly stories that help you own your own excellence.

- Ask for divine assistance.

- Be patient and persistent. Change may not occur as quickly as you'd like.

ACCEPTING AND BESTOWING SUPPORT

No one can heal your painful feelings but you, and it's almost impossible to heal them all by yourself. We all need support especially when our noses are pressed so tightly against the map that we can't see which road to take. Good friends and confidants can offer understanding, compassion, and guidance as well as bringing clear and objective observations to muddled situations.

Isolation kills. We know from studies of orphaned children and animals that babies wither away if they aren't talked to and held frequently. The clinical term for this wasting-away syndrome is "failure to thrive." Without support systems adults, too, fail to thrive.

Support is not one-sided. If we are to receive support, we must support others. Most of us, however, as women, wives, mothers, doctors, secretaries, professors and so on have been more supportive than supported.

A word of caution about accepting and bestowing support. Remember, a healthy source of support cares about our pain but does not carry it for us or try to cure it. Nor can we ever realistically expect to carry or cure another person's pain. We need to be careful not to fall into the trap of either passively expecting others to do all the healing work for us or try to do all the work for someone else.

Watch for signs of an unhealthy imbalance in your support relationships. Fatigue and feeling overloaded by others' troubles or wanting to avoid certain people because you feel impatient or angry with them may signal that you are giving yourself away and not being refilled. Also, seeing these reactions in yourself may mean you're carrying others' pain as if it were your own—perhaps even feeling total responsibility for saving them—a situation that indicates you've neglected to honor your own limits and boundaries.

Conversely, if you feel angry at, abandoned, rejected, victimized, or deserted by your support system (or part of it), ask yourself if you've been expecting them to carry and cure your pain for you. Every person is responsible for his or her own pain. Feel with other people, not for them. Be a care-giver, not a cure-giver.

Expand your support systems. Treat yourself to several sources of comfort and guidance. Finding safe places and safe people with whom you are free to be your real self takes time and requires implicit trust but is a life-enhancing, possibly even a life-saving, quest.

THE ART OF EMOTIONAL MAINTENANCE

Many of us who are drawn to this kind of book have emotionally vulnerable areas that are resistant to change. When a comment or action strikes these vulnerable pockets, our sense of well-being can vanish quick as a wink. It's as if we've been sucked into a pit of emotional quicksand.

Those of us who recognize ourselves in that description—and I am definitely one—are what I call emotionally high maintenance women. Many of us have been afflicted with what Oprah calls the "disease to please" and, because of that and other reasons, are easily affected by others' actions and attitudes toward us. It's important to note that being emotionally high maintenance doesn't necessarily mean that other people feel the need to treat us with kid gloves or even think of us as requiring extraordinary emotional upkeep at all. But *we* are certainly aware of how deeply and quickly we feel; how sensitive we are.

Knowing the extent of our sensitivity, it is our responsibility to take care of ourselves in the most helpful ways. Neither berating ourselves for our weak wimpyness nor casting blame on those who trigger our gut reactions helps us heal. The only effective ways I've found to regain and maintain a sense of emotional well-being and equilibrium is to become aware of our special areas of vulnerability, acknowledge and accept them, and commit to gently and compassionately reassuring and caring for ourselves when they flare.

Naming the fact that I'm emotionally high maintenance has been very healing. For years I slathered myself with guilt because, as a therapist and a woman who's worked on herself for over thirty-five years, I "should know better" and "be above all this." Yee gods, am I ever going to be able to blow it off when someone projects their unfinished business on to me or perceives me as the kind of person I devoutly hope I'm not?! Understanding that the answer is probably "no" is helpful because with that understanding came the realization that my sensitivity is a part of myself that I value and don't want to deny or crust over in an effort to protect myself. In light of that awareness, a few hurt feelings seem an equitable trade-off.

I don't know what your answer will be if you, too, realize you are emotionally high maintenance. It may parallel mine and my need to concentrate on balancing sensitivity with self-love. A large part of balancing self-love and sensitivity is accepting and nurturing myself even when I feeling roundly walloped emotionally. I need to realize and remember that my equilibrium rarely returns without some conscious self-care and patient processing.

An incident happened just the other night, and fortunately I remembered to reassure and restore myself rather than criticize. Driving home, I disidentified with the feelings by saying, "I have this feeling, but I am *not* this feeling. I am a wise and loving child of God."

Pulling out all stops, I used several more techniques we've discussed in the book, talked to my inner child reassuringly, and sang, "God is loving me now" and "I am loving me now." The next day I shared the experience, and what I'd done as a result of it, with my cheerleader friend and my husband, both of whom can be trusted to support me. All of my efforts helped enormously. Realistically I know I'll probably experience similar feelings again. But, thank goodness, that is a reality I can finally accept with love rather than blame.

If you are a sensitive woman, it's important to know that an emotional and bodily response to hurtful people does not necessarily mean you have not forgiven them. It simply means that you retain a cellular memory of a deep vulnerability in this sensitive area. Continuing feelings indicate we are still a work-in-progress and give us yet another opportunity to learn the life-lesson they represent. Ah so, ain't it loverly?!

Observe yourself and others honestly and gently. None of us is "finished" yet, and chances are we won't be finished within this one, short life span. Accept yourself as you are right now and enjoy the process of creating and re-creating yourself. With humor, tolerance, and forgiveness, allow yourself to be transparent to trustworthy and accepting supporters who care for you and for whom you care. Honor yourself and your becomingness. The courage to be yourself is a journey more easily accomplished in a climate of compassion, acceptance, and support.

HONORING YOUR PAST, PRESENT, AND POTENTIAL

Neither our past nor our present indicates our full potential, which is limitless. To open ourselves to our potential, we need to learn from the past, live fully in the present, and look forward to the future.

Our past, whether it was securely nurturing or devastatingly horrible, gives us the building blocks with which we design our lives. If those building blocks are faulty, it is our task to learn the lessons they offer and, as a result, transform them from obstacles to growth into stepping-stones to a more fulfilling present. Recognizing that our accrued wisdom is the result of all the experiences we've had can help us heal as we honor our past and find the courage to embrace the future, no matter what it may hold.

The only moment of life we really have is the present—this minute, this hour, this day. All opportunities beckon us from the center of this moment. Today we can improve on our choices, stand up for our rights, and befriend ourselves. As Elizabeth Barrett Browning so elegantly states, it is up to us to "Light tomorrow with today."

As we work to become truly ourselves, each new day is an opportunity to evolve in the perfect, right way. As a wise and wonderful woman once told me, "The future depends on a healed past and a well-lived present." Honor your present by living this day in a manner that will enable you to look back tomorrow with pride. Choose well today, take good care of yourself, and commit to loving yourself just as you are—unfinished and still learning. As the limiting shackles of fear loosen and an internal sense of balance and harmony develops, you will be able to embrace life with courage and compassion.

Honoring yourself by healing past and present wounds and finding the courage to love and accept yourself now invites your potential to fulfill itself naturally and effortlessly.

LIFE-LESSONS

Mystics, poets, and spiritual teachers assure us that, in the grand scheme of things, each soul is eternal, fear-free, and unlimited. Most of us, however, have amnesia regarding that comforting truth and consequently our individual soulscapes are strewn with life-lessons that invite us to remember.

Accepting that each lesson encountered presents an opportunity to move a step closer to wholeness and be a smidgen better at expressing our real selves helps us embrace rather than resist them. God must have a sense of humor because life-lessons are typically presented by annoying people who grate on our nerves. Of course, they may set our teeth on edge because they come toting invitations to yet another life-lesson party. Lesson-bearers who activate our fears, stir up our insecurities, and frustrate the bejeebers out of us are, in fact, our greatest teachers.

As I've indicated, one of my major life-lessons is self-love. So, naturally, I've drawn people into my life who cannot or will not see me as loving no matter how hard I try to be the Perfect All-Loving Person. Obviously I have a ways to go in learning this particular lesson completely since a dear friend recently said, "I can hardly wait until you can stomp your little Mary Janes and say, 'I don't care what anyone else thinks, I love me!!!'"

Maybe I'll learn self-love fully in this lifetime, maybe I won't. But I have learned three things: to commit to loving myself no matter what, to take care of myself when I'm hurting, and, most importantly, to be grateful for my life-lessons and the teachers who make me face them.

Each adverse circumstance, in fact everything we experience as we trek through our personal soulscapes, can contribute to our soul's growth. Conversely, if we don't face our fears, move through our feelings, and befriend ourselves, each difficult person or circumstance can also contribute to emotional and spiritual atrophy. It's up to us. We have the right to make our own choices.

What life-lessons decorate your soulscape? Who is especially talented at depositing lessons on your doorstep? What circumstances bring you face to face with that which you'd most like to avoid? If you're not sure what your life-lessons are, think about those situations in which you are most vulnerable, or go back over the Woman's Bill of Rights to see if one or two trigger a gut-gripping response in you. Ask your friends. Very often friends can mirror perfectly that which we can't see by ourselves. Also, a kind and competent therapist can help us ferret out life-lessons.

Becoming aware of, acknowledging, and accepting our life-lessons greatly facilitates learning them. As we accept and embrace the natural ebb and flow of our lives and feelings, we can revel in the splendor and power of high tide and discover the wonders revealed in the shallow pools at low tide. Exploring and healing our feelings, whether high or low, brings a treasure beyond belief: the treasure of authenticity.

Our ultimate challenge—the one that requires immeasurable courage—is to trust ourselves, life's process, and the Divine Beloved. Held in the embrace of trust, we will discover the courage to be our true and beautiful selves.

Above all, be gentle with yourself. Enhancing self-esteem and increasing emotional strength happens gradually, step by tiny step. Becoming yourself is a life-long, ever-evolving process.

Mother God, help me to be Loving
Father God, help me to be of Service
Divine Beloved, help me to be Me;
a unique and cherished expression of You.

Acknowledgments

Huge thank yous and many hugs to my dear friends, Bonnie Hampton, who walked the first steps of the original edition of *The Courage to Be Yourself* with me, and Judith Mangus, who was an invaluable idea-giver and cheerleader for this Tenth Anniversary Edition.

I am forever grateful to Julie Bennett who first saw the value of my written work and to the wonderful people at Conari Press—Leslie Berriman, Brenda Knight, Mary Jane Ryan, Sharon Donovan, Heather McArthur, Teresa Coronado, Leah Russell, Rosie Levy, Suzanne Albertson, Claudia Smelser, Pam Suwinsky, and Jenny Collins—who expertly transform my thoughts, words, and dreams into the reality of a book.

For all the inspiration they've given me, a special thank you wings its way to the writers I've quoted within these pages.

A world of gratitude to Gene Thoele, my husband and beloved, for the world of love, humor, security, and support he so enthusiastically provides.

About the Author

Sue Patton Thoele is a licensed psychotherapist and the author of ten books. She and her husband, Gene, live in Colorado, close to their four adult children, son-in-law, and grandsons. Her passions include being with her family, swimming with free dolphins, and encouraging herself and other women in their trek toward self-realization, peace of mind and heart, and creative service. Her other books include:

The Woman's Book of Soul

The Courage to Be a Stepmom

The Woman's Book of Courage

Autumn of the Spring Chicken

The Woman's Book of Confidence

Heart Centered Marriage

The Woman's Book of Spirit

Freedoms After 50

The Courage to Be Yourself Journal

Mango Publishing, established in 2014, publishes an eclectic list of books by diverse authors—both new and established voices—on topics ranging from business, personal growth, women's empowerment, LGBTQ studies, health, and spirituality to history, popular culture, time management, decluttering, lifestyle, mental wellness, aging, and sustainable living. We were recently named 2019 and 2020's #1 fastest-growing independent publisher by *Publishers Weekly*. Our success is driven by our main goal, which is to publish high-quality books that will entertain readers as well as make a positive difference in their lives.

Our readers are our most important resource; we value your input, suggestions, and ideas. We'd love to hear from you—after all, we are publishing books for you!

Please stay in touch with us and follow us at:
    Facebook: Mango Publishing
    Twitter: @MangoPublishing
    Instagram: @MangoPublishing
    LinkedIn: Mango Publishing
    Pinterest: Mango Publishing
    Newsletter: mangopublishinggroup.com/newsletter

Join us on Mango's journey to reinvent publishing, one book at a time.